ARNOLD
EDINBOROUGH

ARNOLD EDINBOROUGH

An autobiography

Stoddart

First published in 1991 by
Stoddart Publishing Co. Limited
34 Lesmill Road
Toronto, Canada
M3B 2T6

Canadian Cataloguing in Publication Data

Edinborough, Arnold,
Arnold Edinborough

ISBN 0-7737-2539-3

1. Edinborough, Arnold, 1922–   . 2. Editors – Canada – Biography.
I. Title.

PN4913.E4A3 1991   07

Cover Design: Leslie Styles
Indexer: Heather Ebbs
Typesetting: Tony Gordon Ltd.
Printed in Canada

CONTENTS

PREFACE

THIS IS A STORY OF TWO YOUNG people who came to shape their lives in a new country. It is also a story of what has happened to the country to which they came.

Canada has changed beyond belief in the past fifty years. As an immigrant from England, I have been an ardent admirer of that change and a passionate participant in it — passionate because I believe in Canada, what it is and what it can be. To that end I have travelled this land from Whitehorse to Windsor, from Stephenville to Port Alberni. I have been involved in education as a university teacher; in church affairs as a lay preacher and speaker; in journalism as the editor of a daily newspaper, the editor and publisher of a national magazine, and columnist for the leading financial weekly. And for the past fifteen years I have built a solid bridge between business and the arts.

I have been involved on the boards of such different and widely separated arts organizations as the Vancouver Playhouse, the Elliot Lake Centre, the New Symphony Association of Kingston, the Stratford Festival, and Roy Thomson and Massey Halls. I have served on such social welfare agency boards as the John Howard Society of Ontario, the Community Information Centre of Metropolitan Toronto, and the Abbeyfield Houses Society of Canada.

My wife, Letitia, founded the Abbeyfield Houses Society of

Canada, was president of St. Christopher House in Toronto, and has been a board member of Bloorview Hospital, the Metropolitan Toronto YWCA, and the federal Consultative Council on Multiculturalism.

We have both acted on the amateur stage and been professionally involved in radio and television. She still, after seventeen years of it, is an active docent at the Royal Ontario Museum.

We have seen theatre in Canada grow from the New Play Society in Toronto and the International Players in Kingston, to a national network of regional, alternative, and dinner theatres involving over a thousand actors at any one time. We have seen a cluster of summer festivals emerge that extend in time from April to November, and in space from Stephenville, Newfoundland, to Nanaimo, British Columbia, with exotic satellites in Dawson City, Whitehorse, Yellowknife, and the northern hinterland of Quebec.

All these changes have affected not only us, but also our family. One daughter now runs a totally nonsubsidized theatre school in London, Ontario. The other is director of communications for the Council for Business and the Arts in Canada. Our son was one of the founders of the arts and poetry festival at Upper Canada College; two grandsons are professional actors, one in television (*The Road to Avonlea*), the other in theatre (at Young People's Theatre in Toronto). They have all been part of the adventure and each has a personal stake in this country, the changes in which, over the past fifty years, have been the biggest adventure of all.

I

TO THE
NEW WORLD

W E DID NOT ARRIVE IN CANADA, my wife and I, until 1947. Up to then Canada was not much more than a name to us. I at least had a family connection. My father's younger brother had gone to Saskatchewan in 1907 and had homesteaded on the prairie. An unlettered man, his correspondence with his brother was rare. As a boy, I remember seeing grainy photographs of young cousins wearing woollen hats, large mittens, and heavy coats, sitting on the steps of a wooden house, the surrounding area deep in snow. My wife's connection was even slimmer: her uncle had left the Outer Hebrides in the late days of the last century, sailed to Canada, and had never been heard of since.

As children we were not worried about such family occurrences. They were outside our sphere. Letitia grew up in Spalding, Lincolnshire, a market town of some nine thousand people. Her father's family had been cabinetmakers for three generations. We have a butler's tray and a monk's bench here in Canada made in her great-grandfather's workshops. Her mother — a Hebridean from North Uist — had left the islands to be companion to Letitia Hale-Hilton, a wealthy distant aunt who had left her enough money to pay for her children's education in such extra accomplishments as music and dancing, and enough class-consciousness to see that they did not speak in the same Lincolnshire dialect as their classmates at the local (but fee-paying) high school.

I was pure Lincolnshire. My father owned a small farm that, together with his wife and two sons, he ran himself. We grew potatoes as a cash crop, plus wheat and oats to feed our own livestock. They consisted of pigs, a dozen dairy cows, and two workhorses. All my relatives were farmers. None had ever gone beyond village school (the equivalent of grade eight). Like them, when I attended the village school, I came home every afternoon to do chores: chopping the mangolds and turnips, mucking out the pigs and horses, carrying in the bedding for the cows that my father would be milking. My older (and only) brother was set to become a farmer also, and did. But a gypsy had come to our farmhouse door one day and, after selling clothes pegs to my mother, looked at me, so my mother used to say, and declared, "That boy will never be a farmer. He will be an inspector of inspectors of schools."

The gypsy's vision did not impress me: money, muck, and tates (Lincolnshire for potatoes) was my destiny, I thought. And yet I revelled in the books my mother and father read to me. I learned them by heart so that they mistakenly thought I could read long before I actually could. And when I got to the village school, I found the same excitement in what two notable women teachers read to us, or caused us to read for ourselves.

At the age of ten, therefore, I was groomed by the headmaster to take the entrance examination for the grammar school in Spalding, an Elizabethan foundation of 1588. To my surprise I not only won a place, I won a scholarship. My fees would be paid and, despite the Depression, my mother insisted that she would, out of the meagre farm income, see to it that I had the school uniform, the extra gear for games, and other necessary things. A better bicycle to go the four miles there and back every day was no problem. I had raided one of our early potato crops, weighed the new potatoes into six-pound bags, and sold them in the village for a shilling a piece. Two weekends brought in thirty shillings, which bought me a Raleigh bicycle with a three-speed Sturmey-Archer gear.

The two women who had sparked my interest at the West Pinchbeck Cowley and Brown Endowed School, the village school's proper name, were now superseded by two masters at the grammar school: the classics master and the English teacher.

Arnold Bottomley, the classics master, was passionate about amateur theatre, and he produced a Shakespeare or other classic English play every year. In the true Shakespearean tradition he relied on young boys with unbroken voices to play the women's parts. In my third year at the school, voice still unbroken at thirteen, I was chosen to play Katherina in *The Taming of the Shrew*. It was an exhilarating experience. For three nights the audience of parents, uncles, cousins, and aunts lapped it up.

Each night, as a normally grubby, fat junior boy, I knelt in front of the captain of the school, playing Petruchio, and said with feeling in my white Elizabethan wedding dress:

> *Then vail your stomachs, for it is no boot,*
> *And place your hands below your husband's foot;*
> *In token of which duty, if he please,*
> *My hand is ready, may it do him ease.*

In my mind I placed my hand below Shakespeare's foot. Plays, not potatoes, became my burning ambition, and Bottomley's skill in erasing my Lincolnshire accent and giving me "standard" English speech, made the aspiration a good deal more feasible.

The other teacher, Dr. James Goode, was an English instructor who recognized my passion for Shakespeare and the spoken word. The year I was fifteen he took me aside. "Not many of our people go to Cambridge, Edinborough. You have the talent and ambition to get there. So let's do it."

Looking back now, I see that he and Bottomley, quietly, persistently, almost covertly, worked to that end.

Literally on the other side of the fence that separated the High School for Girls from the Grammar School for Boys, Letitia Woolley was following a different path. Athletic, competitive, she shone more on the playing field than in the classroom. She was soon tennis champion of the school and a bronze medallist in diving and swimming at the interschool meet in Peterborough in her senior year. Doing the reverse of what I had done, she had played male roles in the girls' drama productions: Dunois in Shaw's *Saint Joan*, Malvolio in *Twelfth Night*. She also played the cello in the school orchestra.

We met by design, though both denied it. A rare interschool tennis match was arranged. I put my name down for it and was surprised to find Letitia Woolley had picked me as her doubles partner. I was a moderate player only; she was the champion. There was more in this, I thought, than tennis. She saved our match from being a rout by superb play. I knew at the end of the tournament that she was the girl I would marry.

Goode and Bottomley did their jobs well. I got almost enough scholarships to pay my way to Cambridge in October 1940. The gap of thirty pounds my father, who was just as eager for me to go but cautious of his income (he could not have survived the Depression had he not been), was directed by my mother to find. Against Bottomley, Goode, the gypsy, my mother, and me, he had no choice.

I arrived in Cambridge, immediately auditioned for the Marlowe Society which, despite its name, produced mainly Shakespeare's plays, and landed the part of Elbow in *Measure for Measure*. This was the big world for me. My fellow players were all from the great English public schools: Rugby, Eton, Harrow, Winchester. But Bottomley had done his work well. I had learned how to act and speak as well as any of them, and Goode, with his long and personal supervision, had brought me to an understanding of the plays that even some of my new acquaintances did not have.

Letty, a games girl, was not likely to come to Cambridge, which before 1940 was a man's university. Only very bright, academically determined women were encouraged to apply, and even then they were sequestered in two out-of-the-way colleges, miles from the centre of the university proper. The war, now beginning to get serious, intervened on her behalf. She wanted to train as a physiotherapist, but the course was too expensive for her father, whose business was in a war-depression (why buy today what might get bombed tomorrow?). So she opted to train as a nurse. Normally that would mean at Guy's or St. Bartholomew's Hospitals in London. But the blitz needed trained nurses, not students. And she therefore came to Addenbrookes Hospital at Cambridge, and we were together again.

The same war sent me off to the army soon after she arrived, and out to North Africa not long after that. Not before, though, we had become engaged without parental consent, she being nineteen, I being twenty. Consent came at twenty-one, not that we really were concerned. We had known we were engaged, anyway, and there is a six-inch-thick file of letters to and from each other throughout the next four years.

Those letters make nostalgic reading now. They chronicle the day-by-day events of one man's war. Some are full of lovesick longing; others are high-spirited, carefully self-censored accounts of various military engagements. There are even references to an Italian girl who briefly became a possible substitute for the girl I was writing to. But mainly they talk of the future, a future we knew would be shared. And so, in fact, it turned out.

By December 1945 I was home from the Mediterranean, discharged as a captain from the army, and returned to my college in Cambridge. In January 1946 we were married and set up house in rented rooms. It was an unbelievably rich time for both of us. We had money from my ex-service allowance. We had time for me to get my degree. We were now *both* in the Marlowe Society, spouses being allowed in under the ex-service conditions. I was rowing in the varsity and college boat, acting in the Marlowe Society, was president of the Footlights Club, and had a very different attitude to my courses. If I had been four years away from, say, mathematics or natural sciences, I would have found the gap perhaps too much to catch up on before my first examinations. But in English literature I now brought an adult experience, and a heightened wartime experience at that, to bear on what I was reading. The army staff college, truncated though my course had been, had also taught me analysis and a lucid style. And being in charge — total charge — of the life and death of two hundred men had taught me to strip away nonessentials and to shape disparate events into a recognizable, realizable goal.

Letty's training had done much the same for her. At twenty-one she had become sister-in-charge of a forty-bed ward for women with septicemia, some of the cases being attributable to botched abortions. She had coped with hideously wounded airmen from local airfields and routinely laid out the one or two patients who expired every night. She was compassionate, experienced, gifted with organizational ability, and brimming with energy, gusto, and mirth.

If it sounds like Arcadia, it was, for we had both realized, almost simultaneously, that these two years in Cambridge might be the happiest we would ever spend, equipped as we were with friends, money, time, and all the eagerness of young love so long deferred.

So they proved. Friends made then are still the people we see after a separation of forty years and thousands of miles. The memorable occasions — the balls, the dinners, the walks in the countryside, the concerts, the theatre, evenings with tutors and dons (once Olympian presences in college but now family friends) — were made all the more memorable for us all because we had dreamed that they might happen, dreamed about them in lonely outposts in the Western Desert, or on the long runs home from bombing raids over Germany, or in the dogwatches of the Murmansk convoys. And we, we happy few, had been spared to see the dream come true.

There was a dark side: the war, with its pulverizing bombing raids, had left the country short of housing. Finding a place to live was time-consuming, expensive, and distressing. The fire sale of foreign assets had left the U.K. with a shortage of hard international currency. The run-down transportation system, having been used ruthlessly for war purposes, made even food distribution difficult.

We had also discovered that university teachers' salaries in England were so low as to be laughable. They seemed to be still based on the assumption that such teachers would, like their medieval predecessors, be unmarried and live in college, their room and board provided, their salary being merely pocket money.

Or else the salaries were based on an equally mistaken assumption that the people aspiring to the profession were younger sons of the landed classes who had their way to make, but with the help of a modest yet significant private income. (My brigadier, before sending me back to Cambridge, had asked if I had a private income. When I said no, he said, "Pity, because if you had I would have tried to keep you in the regiment. You are a good soldier.")

Furthermore, those landed classes, despite two wars, still existed, and their network assured that the plum jobs were shaken off the appointments tree more by connections than merit.

"I think," I had said one day to Letty, "when I graduate we might go abroad for a couple of years until things sort themselves out."

Letty, fed up with coping as a neophyte cook with bizarre recipes based on the powdered milk, dried egg, and butcher's offal that were still the staples of a postwar rationed economy, agreed.

It was not a philosophical decision. We did not fulminate against the newly elected Labour government. We did not think "they" (whoever "they" were) were against us. It was just a simple housekeeping decision.

We spread our net wide. Interviews with the British Council elicited job offers in Belo Horizonte, Brazil, and in Istanbul. They were strange offers: in both cases Letty was also part of the package. In Brazil she would teach physical training; in Turkey she would help to train hospital aides.

Our ideas about these particular jobs were somewhat dashed by my meeting at a college dinner one night Sir Campbell Stuart, a Canadian who was general manager of the *Times*. "British Council," he said. "Ronnie Adams's boys." (General Sir Ronald Adams had been made chairman of the council on retirement.) "High thinking and low living. Large concepts and small salaries. Wouldn't go near 'em."

Another lead came from my tutor, Tom Henn. He said they needed a lecturer in English literature at the University of Colombo in Ceylon. He thought I might do. He himself, he reminisced, had been in India for a few years after graduation and before St. Catharine's College had invited him back as a fellow.

I pondered what he had said. Was he hinting that after a few years in Ceylon there might be a fellowship on the horizon for me? Me, a don at Cambridge? High table, old claret, good talk, and infinite tenure. We discussed it that evening. But my record, almost a first class but not quite, seemed to lean more to Colombo than Cambridge.

And then a breakthrough. G. B. Harrison, eminent Shakespearean scholar, diarist, popularizer and yet solid academic, then expatriate head of the English department at Queen's University in Kingston, Ontario, wrote to Henn. Did he, he asked, have anyone interested in drama and the like who might have had some experience in teaching (even if only at the seminar level) and was prepared to make a career outside the United Kingdom?

I had mentioned to Henn that a time out of England might suit us. He knew of my work with the Marlowe Society. He had personally recommended me to teach summer school in English language and literature at the University of Lausanne in Switzerland. There, in such distinguished company as Stephen Spender the poet, the minister of education in Clement Attlee's government, and George Kitson-Clarke, a constitutional historian from Trinity College, I had already had experience in university teaching.

Henn recommended me to Harrison, but with that genial but irritating insouciance of Cambridge dons, forgot to tell me. The first I knew about it was an envelope in my pigeonhole at the porter's lodge, which contained a letter to Henn with a cryptic note attached to me: "Arnold Edinborough: pse see & note." The letter was from G. B. Harrison, who said that Queen's was "interested" in me and gave some details of what I might find if I were to follow the matter up:

> *Anyone coming here must be prepared to come with an open mind, for he will find many things quite strange and different from what he has ever met before. Standards are lower, but the students are keener, and very friendly. Far more lecturing, but not more than twelve hours a week in the classroom; and what a man does outside in the way of personal contacts is his own concern.*
>
> *The year runs from about 25 September to 7 April with ten days' break at Christmas; then a month of examinations, etc.*
>
> *From the beginning of May until the following September, a man is free to do what he likes, but we do naturally expect that he will not spend the whole time fishing. . . .*

Progress and promotion depend on teaching ability and — this is important — a man being something more than a mere teacher; but in Canada promotion is a matter of merit and not of waiting about for a vacancy and joining the circus of people who run around trying to get a chair.

In my department at present we have three full professors and shall have four next October.

There were then some specific instructions as to how to meet with Dr. R. C. Wallace, the principal of Queen's, who would be in London at the end of May. Harrison ended:

It would be as well for Edinborough to ask me all the questions that he feels desirable and write frankly, for I would not wish him to have any sense of awful disillusion. Canada is not, as is wrongly supposed, a country of vast and progressive ideas. On the contrary, when I first arrived [he had gone out in 1942], I felt that I had stepped back into my Victorian childhood.

I wrote instantly. God knows I had plenty of questions. I knew so little that I addressed the letter to Kingston, Toronto. But Harrison was not dismayed by such ignorance, and his replies to me were as frank as his initial letter had been to Henn.

Kingston was, he said, a small provincial town. What cultural activities there were, were made by the people themselves. Montreal and Toronto, though better, were not London (or Cambridge, for that matter), but they were fairly accessible. But we would miss a lot.

Twelve hours of lectures a week seemed enormous from a Cambridge standpoint where professors lectured once or at most twice a week. But then Queen's had no tutorials as such, and perhaps the total work load was not as heavy as it might seem. I would enjoy the students, he said, but not, at first, the townspeople, who were Scottish by heritage and dourly Presbyterian in temperament. He thought, however, that Canada in general and Queen's in particular was on "the edge of a renaissance."

The salary would be the equivalent of six hundred pounds per year (half as much again as for a comparable post in England), and though housing and clothes were dearer, income tax was much less.

He closed on a positive and welcoming note: "I hope you'll have a happy time with us."

I made arrangements to meet Dr. Wallace in London, as Harrison suggested. He was a spare, tallish man with an attractive Scottish burr. Very friendly, eager to put me at my ease, and most apologetic about the difficulties of lunch at the partly bombed Atheneum Club. I remember that he had a grilled herring, "since you can't get fish worth calling fish in Kingston," and that we had to move to other chairs for coffee since the rain came in through the damaged roof where we first sat down.

He talked about the university. A Scottish foundation with original links to the University of Edinburgh (appropriate in my case, he said with a twinkle), it had in its first fifty years or so been controlled by the Presbyterian Church but that attachment had been cut sometime since. It was a smallish but, by Canadian standards, old university, founded in 1842, with a family feeling about it that I might find reminiscent of, but in no way comparable to, Cambridge.

At the time we met we talked about an appointment in which I would teach public speaking and drama within the English department. He could not at that moment, however, make me a firm offer, but he would be in touch.

He was not in touch all through May. But we were too busy to notice.

The early summer of 1947 was one of the best England could remember. One cloudless blue-sky day followed another in unbelievable succession. Cambridge, ancient university city that it was, had never looked lovelier, especially to the eyes of those of us who had seen city after city reduced to rubble in the previous five years. The college May Balls were exhilarating, and our youthful stamina had seen us at three or four such dusk-to-dawn affairs in succession.

As I lazily punted us up the river to Grantchester after the Jesus College Ball, the sun rising, the river steaming, I remember thinking how lucky I was just to be alive, let alone alive in that idyllic spot. For in the eighteen months in which I had returned from overseas, married, and finished my degree, the war had been still very much with us. Most of the undergraduates were ex-service men. Some were maimed or crippled, and a handful of ex-fighter pilots were hideously disfigured by burns. One member of my own college had gone completely berserk; another acquaintance had jumped to his death on the cobbles from the roof of the college where his father was master.

The easy rhythm of lectures and libraries and essays had been healing. So was, in the English department, the stuff we read.

But the best part of coming back for many of us was marriage. The gradual relief from nightmares and the sudden chilling vision of dead men's faces came from love not literature.

Finally a letter came from Orkney House, Kirkwall, the Orkney Islands. Dated June 13, 1947, it read:

Dear Mr. Edinborough:

I am advised by cable that, owing to a resignation, there is now a definite vacancy for full-time work in the department of English at Queen's. I will be in a position consequently to offer you an appointment, subject to the two-year arrangement for all appointments, as a lecturer in English. Whatever you might do in dramatics or public speaking would be incidental, and accord-

ing to your own inclinations, though very acceptable. If at the end of two years there is mutual satisfaction, the appointment will be made permanent at salary and rank to be decided at that time. I would suggest for the two-year period a salary of $2,600 per year, beginning on September 1, in order that you might have a month's salary before teaching duties begin and to assist in travelling expenses.

I hope that you will now make definite arrangements for passage and that we can get together when I return on June 25 to discuss all details.

With warm regards,
Very sincerely yours,
Rob C. Wallace

We were committed to leaving England now. We had, as Wallace said, to make "definite arrangements."

We had been living in half a house on Huntingdon Road, shared with a mathematics scholar from Trinity whose closest friend was Christopher Robin Milne, the Christopher Robin of *Winnie-the-Pooh*. Even with the stringencies that government grants imposed, we had amassed a fair number of books, some pictures, and a collection of such usual college memorabilia as oars, coaching crests, team pictures, and the like.

How to get all this stuff safely across the Atlantic was a problem, especially when Harrison had made a point of saying several times: "bring all the books you can." I made the rounds of secondhand shops and eventually found what a variety of moving men learned to curse roundly in the next few years — two sheet steel army document boxes, fireproof and otherwise impregnable, measuring six feet long, two feet wide, and two feet deep. Packed with books, they weighed about three hundred pounds a piece.

Everything else was finally stowed in my old college trunk and a venerable bass, a sort of wickerwork hamper covered in leather that had been around the Edwardian world with Aunt Letitia Hale-Hilton, who had given my wife her name and her mother her luggage.

Our last meeting with Tom Henn was moving. He told us how the postwar crop of men had been "a vintage lot" and how much he had enjoyed working with us. He invented a pretext to get me out of the room and gave some good advice to Letty as well as praising her for her understanding role in the previous eighteen months when I had often been much busier and more preoccupied than any newly married man should be. He then broke out a bottle of gin instead of the inevitable college sherry, and we bid each other a somewhat moist farewell.

At the house we had one last boozy roundup of rowing men and others. All the liquor we could find was tipped into an earthenware puncheon labelled Drink: Mark I (and II, then finally III as the evening progressed to the next morning).

Then Cambridge was over.

We had one more meeting with Douglas Eves, our closest friend, in London; a couple of weeks or so at home in Lincolnshire where only one wise old aunt twigged that Letty was pregnant; and then, on August 27, 1947, we boarded the SS *Aquitania* at Southampton and headed for Canada.

The second night out, leaning over the rail, looking at the wake streaming back to England, and thinking of what the previous twenty-five years there had been like for us both, Letty suddenly said, "I feel so lonely. Who knows what the future will bring? Have we cut ourselves off? Have we done the right thing?"

Who knew?

I took refuge, as I have so often, in someone else's words. They are by Arthur Hugh Clough, a Victorian poet whose work my mother knew even in village school:

And not by eastern windows only,
When daylight comes, comes in the light,
In front the sun climbs slow, how slowly,
But westward, look, the land is bright.

And westward for the next five days we steamed until one morning we woke up in Halifax.

II

ANTICLIMAX IN KINGSTON

H AD WE LOOKED AT HALIFAX WITH a less romantic eye we would no doubt have seen, even at first glance, that it was dirty, run-down, and exhausted by the never-ending convoys it had put together and dispatched during four years of war. But this was America — the continent we had only read about, seen on films, and fantasized about.

We knew it immediately from the dress of two workmen rebuilding a roof on the wharf: neat-fitting overalls and a peaked cap. Every film we had ever seen had taught us that.

We were soon ashore, watching our luggage thump onto the dock. And in no time North American marketing and enterprise had collared us.

"We took this picture as you came into dock this morning," a man said. "Souvenir of your first sight of Canada and your trip here."

It was, of course, a stock shot of the *Aquitania* taken who knows when. But we bought it, as did almost everybody else as they waited for porters to handle their luggage.

It had been a somewhat stormy voyage, but we had made good friends, two of whom we still see from time to time, even though they are at opposite ends of the country: John Chapman and his wife, Pat, were on their way to the University of British Columbia, where he recently retired as head of the geography department after the forty intervening years. Ron Baker, off to UBC as a student, now the retired founding president of the University of Prince Edward Island.

We had a little time before the boat train to Montreal left.

"Since I'm here," Letty said, "I'm going to have an Andy Hardy banana split. All through the war and its rationing I yearned for one as he and his friends ate them in the film."

The dock area of Halifax in 1947 was not a good place to try it. But we went into a soda fountain, a good deal downscale from Andy Hardy's haunts.

I can see that banana split now: two long slices of browning banana, two scoops of stiff ice cream, a huge dollop of canned whipped cream, topped by half a cherry and a spoonful of crumbled nuts, the whole thing swimming in a sauce malevolently red in colour and cloyingly sweet to the taste. Even Letty, starved of sugar and cream through seven years of rationed war and English peace, gave up. We walked back to the boat train, pondering whether other ideas would be equally far from reality in this new land of ours.

About midnight the train left. We looked forward to streaking across the great open spaces of Canada. In England boat trains are the monarchs of the iron road. When a boat train once starts, everything else gets out of the way to let it through. We had been on the Golden Arrow together only a year before — a train people stood in their fields to watch as it flew by. I had even made one exotic trip from Paris to Trieste on the old Simplon Express.

Canadian boat trains, we discovered, were something else. Being an extra (and perhaps also because it was full of war brides and other assorted displaced persons), it was just a nuisance on the throughway. Whenever a regular train, even a freight, got within two sections of it, we pulled onto a siding to let the regular train go by. We once gave way for almost half an hour to two maintenance men who pumped *their* way by us on their tiny platform.

Nor were there the wide-open spaces we had had in our mind's eye. Nothing but mile after mile of scrubby second-growth trees, crowding down towards the rails as we inched our way across the forests of New Brunswick down into Maine and eventually into Quebec. Almost forty-eight hours later we made it to Montreal, our clothes bespattered with the chocolate from hundreds of grubby fingers. All the newly Canadian kids of harassed travelling war brides had been indulging the same craving for sweetness that had driven Letty to the banana split.

At Montreal we paused half a day before getting into another boat train. This would take us only to Kingston, but some poor distracted mothers were en route to Vancouver. By now we had learned enough to book ourselves a bedroom. The overnight trip was going to be comfortable and private — more like the kind of travel we had visualized.

We looked for a long time out of the window at the smoke streaming by, at the great full harvest moon that rose on our left, and went to bed late. What seemed to be our first sleep was broken by the porter knocking at the door saying, "Kingston in five minutes."

Five minutes or not we had to put a proper face on it. Must shave. Letty must make up. But before we got very far with either operation the train stopped. "Kingston, sir. Kingston."

I put my panic-stricken, lather-covered face out the door.

"It's okay, sir. Don't hurry. We'll wait. Plenty of time."

Whether, in fact, he did tell the trainman who did tell the engineer or whether they were taking on water or waiting for a slow freight train to slither by to Gananoque Junction, I shall never know. They did wait, though. We emerged bright and shining some ten minutes later. The porter waved goodbye. The engine rattled its pistons and wheezed westward, taking, we realized as we looked at the empty platform, all our bags except for our hand baggage.

Anticlimax. There was no one there to meet us. There was no one in the station. Trains came into Kingston, normal trains, that is, we later discovered twice a day: at noon and around six in the evening. Trains at other times were nontrains.

So there was no one in the ticket office. There was no one in the baggage room to report that our baggage had gone on west on the boat train. There were no taxis. Worst of all, there was no town.

G. B. Harrison had told us a great deal about our new home, but he had not mentioned that the station at Kingston was called the outer station because it was then on the outskirts of the town.

Letty decided to go to the toilet. Inside she found a woman in her sixties scrubbing the floor.

"'Allo, luv. You just got off that special?"

"Yes."

"So did I, thirty years ago. And look at me now. Worst day's work I ever did. If I could get the money together, wild 'orses couldn't 'old me 'ere in this god-awful country."

Shaken, Letty emerged, but I had by now telephoned a taxi, and it was waiting with our cases already in what he called the trunk and I had called the boot, to his utter astonishment.

"Take us," I said, feeling that only a display of opulence would neutralize Mrs. Mop's gloomy picture of our chances, "to the best place in town for breakfast."

"Check," he said. (I knew what *that* meant from being with the U.S. Army in North Africa.)

We drove through the industrial perimeter of Kingston, passing the tannery (quite a whiff on a humid summer morning), the cement works, a tumbledown stadium, two lumberyards, and an ancient cemetery. Finally we swung into Princess Street and drew up at the best breakfast place in town — the United Cigar Store. We weren't immediately persuaded that it was, but the row of little horse-box cubicles, the smell of coffee and toast, encouraged us.

And whether it was the best or not, the cornflakes came with cream, the bacon was lean, the eggs large and just right. Over the latter we had another language lesson. After a few false moves, we had finally agreed with the waitress that what we wanted was, as she shouted down the counter, "Bacon crisp and two easy over." The coffee was very good. The cream seemed to us rich and thick. Our cups were filled as soon as we emptied them. The toast dripped with butter.

So, breakfasted, awake, polished, and shiny, I went to the telephone again and dialled the number we had been given by Harrison in case meeting arrangements should go, as they had, awry.

Within a very short while Alastair Walker, the next junior man in the English department and a member of one of Canada's most successful business families (his grandfather had helped to found the Bank of Commerce and then the Royal Ontario Museum from its profits), turned up to collect us.

He drove us over to the university where the first student we saw was wearing a bright, shiny red windbreaker with the legend Queen's Arts 50 in large letters across the back. Alastair, who was a graduate both of the University of Toronto and also of Cambridge, interpreted this strange sight. He told us also of the year system, of the different faculties, the different colours of jackets they wore, and the sort of interfaculty rivalry that existed. "It's kind of the North American equivalent to the college colours blazer," he said valiantly.

He then took us over to Professor William Angus, another junior member of the department, to whose house we were invited for dinner that evening. Then, picking up groceries on the way, he drove us to 20 Lower William Street to the apartment that had been engaged for us by G. B. Harrison.

Anyone who ever lived for a short while in Kingston in the 1940s and 1950s, whether as a student or faculty member at

Queen's, or at the Royal Military College, or as an army man stationed in Kingston at any of the various military schools and institutions that abound there, will know that address. It was one of the apartments owned at that time by Mrs. Webb, a redoubtable woman who owned the Belvedere Hotel, 20 and 30 Lower William Street, and a number of other somewhat small and over-furnished apartments in the decaying downtown area of Kingston's waterfront.

Our only window in the living room looked out over an abandoned graveyard whose headstones were piled irregularly in one corner. Through the glass top of the outside door we looked straight into a slaughterhouse where, the very next day, a truck drove up to collect the hides from that month's slaughtering. Another smaller truck, owned by a drover, dropped in the following morning, too, to bring large tubs of otherwise unusable parts of the animals he had killed to be rendered — a process that is hot and smelly to begin with, and we had hit Kingston on one of the hottest and most humid days of the 1947 summer.

Inside, the furniture was shabby, the colour of the wallpaper gravy-brown, the electric stove and fridge of a primitive, quite un-North American kind. In the bathroom there was a terrible smell. We traced it to a paper bag neglected by the previous occupants when they left. It was full of used female sanitary napkins.

That was the final straw. Letty sat down on the bed and wept. I didn't wonder.

"Maybe Belo Horizonte would have been better," she said. "At least we wouldn't have expected so much and been so disappointed."

But the Anguses were kind that evening. The graveyard was dark and therefore unseen by the time we got home. We were sure the morning would be better.

It was. We unpacked, but found there was very little we could do in the way of breakfast since we had no cutlery. It was all packed in the bass, still, as far as we knew, swaying westward on the boat train.

I took my courage in both hands and went around to our neighbours on the other side of the apartment building. They not only lent us forks and such, they insisted we come to breakfast, which they were just cooking. "Sausages, pancakes, and maple syrup," the wife said.

I went to collect Letty. "Oh, yes," she said, "and no doubt for lunch they will have sardines in chocolate sauce sprinkled with hundreds and thousands. Come on!"

But sausages, pancakes, and maple syrup it was. And as Ivy Morgan, who cooked it, asked, "What's the difference between Canadian sausages and maple syrup and England's mutton and red currant jelly or, for that matter, pork and apple sauce?"

She was right. The new land was certainly proving to be new. The Morgans, the Greens from the apartment upstairs, and the Foresters from just over the way were determined that a Mrs. Webb locale wasn't going to be the real welcome to Canada.

"Jesus," Ivy said, "even Canadian army people think these apartments are crummy. If we could find anywhere else to live, we would. But it's not forever, thank God."

And with that, and with a bottle of rye that evening and an invitation to steaks the next day, Kingston began to look better.

The following Tuesday (it being Labour Day on Monday, about which we were also uninformed), I went back to the station to collect our baggage, which had now come back from the West. I collected it, paid the transfer man, then walked down to the end of the platform to get the bus back to town. In front of me two of the most enormous women I have ever seen were hanging naked over the back of a grey-green canvas-covered truck. They were screaming and still throwing other solid articles of clothing after the first, their melonlike breasts flopping around alarmingly.

I asked my seat companion what was going on.

"Doukhobors," he said cryptically. "Going to the pen."

They penned women here? And what did they have to do to deserve it? What were Doukhobors?

I nodded, mystified. There were depths to this country not yet plumbed — not by a long way.

III

CULTURE SHOCK
IN ACADEME

T HE UNIVERSITY ITSELF, EVEN though we had become somewhat acclimatized to Kingston's version of Canada by the
time term started two weeks after our arrival, was a real culture
shock.

For a start, there were far more women than men on campus —
pretty young women, too, who rubbed shoulders with their male
counterparts without any strain. Cambridge women were salted
away in separate colleges and were excessively studious or they
would never have made it. Cambridge men had, by and large,
come from all-boys schools and were either blindingly shy or
blunderingly gauche in their attitude towards the opposite sex.

And there were certain tribal rituals at Queen's that were totally
alien to a newcomer. The hazing of frosh — the imposed task of
selling toilet paper on Kingston street corners, of blacking half
the face during daylight hours, of pinning one side of the skirt up
to the top of the thigh, and other such torments — all seemed
civilizations away from my own freshman days. I had been given
a suite of rooms of my own, a gown, an academic mortar board,
and a list of lectures to go to under the supervision of a nationally,
even internationally known scholar to whom I took an essay on
my own once a week and read it to him (or her).

Having, with the resilience of youth, taken these external curiosities in stride, I did have qualms about what would happen inside the classroom. For my work for these first two years was to be exclusively with the freshman year — a course in the arts faculty and a course in the science faculty. I was to give three lectures a week to each of two arts groups and two lectures a week to each of three science groups.

The science students were actually engineering students who would go out, when trained by Queen's, to mine the resources, build the roads and bridges, erect the buildings, pulp the forests, and generally make Canada work. It was a distinguished tradition. Nearly every mine in Ontario at that time had a Queen's graduate as manager. A Queensman ran one of the national railroads; others were in senior positions at Inco, C-I-L, Alcan, and so on. They kept, as all Queen's alumni did (and do), a fairly close contact with their alma mater, and that clubbiness rubbed off on those young students who often came from the resource-rich but remote north. Such a strong sense of solidarity led to excesses: within the first three weeks of term I had seen them invade and disrupt lectures in the arts building, march through the streets of Kingston in a way, for me, all too easily reminiscent of the Hitler Youth, and pelt the principal, Dr. Wallace, with tomatoes as he walked from his house on campus to his office.

Within the classroom, however, they were controlled by certain tough restraints. Attendance was taken at all lectures, and unless there was eighty percent attendance at the end of term the student could not write his term exam and thus automatically failed his year. Despite that, the students were pretty inured against English as a subject. Calculus, surveying, maths — these were real subjects to them. The writing of English was a pain; the reading of English (in order to learn how to write) an eccentric waste of time.

"I think," I said one morning to Alastair Walker as we went over to Carruthers Hall to each give our classes, "that I'm going to find teaching English at this level in this atmosphere a real problem."

"In England," he said, "it would be thought of as a problem. Here we consider it a challenge."

It was the first time I had ever heard what later became one of the more irritating clichés of Canadian life.

The arts students were a much less purposeful bunch. Half of the girls were there to get a husband — and for some of them three years in a community that had a ratio of four males to one female was not a bit too long for the search. But they were, as Harrison had said they were, a very friendly lot. Sixty-five of them turned up in each of my two sections of English II, a course that went from Beowulf to Virginia Woolf in seventy-two lectures.

There was a set text — an enormous anthology called *The College Survey of English Literature*, consisting of over a thousand thin pages. The book, even in those days, cost fifteen dollars. By the end of the first term the new black briefcase Letty had given me was hopelessly out of shape and its side seams split. Every day from the small apartment in Lower William to Queen's it went back and forth with a ring binder of notes, the anthology (plus a similar one for the science students), and a sheaf of essays.

If the students were different, the members of the department were certainly a bizarre bunch. The head was G. B. Harrison, a man of erudition, of international reputation, but of no tact whatsoever.

The day after I arrived in Kingston the old students' union burned down. This, I discovered, was a source of joy rather than dismay. The insurance would cover a good deal of the cost of building a better and more convenient union.

Harrison went into the vice principal's office the following day and suggested that such a new union might be designed to include an Elizabethan theatre. (Those were the days when J. Cranford Adams and Leslie Hotson had just published their new and exciting studies about the shape of Shakespeare's Globe Theatre in Elizabethan London.)

"Such a theatre," Harrison is alleged to have said, "would put Queen's on the map."

The vice principal, Dr. W. E. MacNeill, a precise and frugal man, though of wide cultivation and with a mind well stored with the great passages of literature (he had been in the English department for some years before he became first treasurer and then vice principal of the university), looked coldly at Harrison.

"I had thought, Professor Harrison," he said, "that Queen's was already on the map."

It is from that interview, I think, that Harrison's interest in Queen's began to decline, and it was the unimaginative, pragmatically mediocre handling of the new union design that eventually led Harrison to leave Queen's two years later to go to the University of Michigan. But of that, more later.

The next senior man in the department was Henry Alexander, a bright linguistics man who had edited an edition of Spenser when very young. From Liverpool originally, he had been at Queen's for thirty years, teaching Anglo-Saxon, Middle English, and such. A nervous man, he had the habit of smoking cigars through meetings and punctuating his speech and that of other people by constantly spitting out the tobacco left on his tongue by the disintegrating end of the cigar. He was a difficult man, too, and still resented the fact that Harrison had been brought in to head the department when he had been clearly in line.

The other senior man was Professor James A. Roy, a small, very fat man who had the strange capacity of balancing his teacup and saucer on his belly while sitting upright in a chair. He was a Scot who had written a book called *The Heart is Highland* and had no intention of staying at Queen's if he could get back to Scotland. His wife had had the same idea and had returned to Scotland years before. He was now a hard-drinking, jolly man whose students adored him. He taught (what else?) Romantic literature, and even in his obese state he was a romantic figure.

The romantic image was heightened by stories of how he had driven his car one night while drunk and ended up in the Kingston jail to which the next senior member of the department had brought his breakfast.

This person was one of the great originals I have ever met. Her name was Wilhelmina Gordon — Minnie to any Queensman who ever took a course from her. Under a wild mass of grey hair she had a long face with a prominent, acromegalic chin — a chin thrust out in many a fight of principle. She was the daughter of a previous principal of Queen's. Unmarried, active in the Imperial Order Daughters of the Empire, devoted to king and country, the Presbyterian Church (the Continuing Presbyterian Church from which people of lesser fibre had gone off to join with the Methodists and Congregationalists in the United Church), and an almost sexual passion for John Milton.

The first time she met me she said, "You're from Cambridge, I hear. What do you think of that dreadful man Leavis?" (F. R. Leavis, the founder of *Scrutiny* and leader of the opposition to the reigning English Faculty at Cambridge in my day.)

"Dreadful," I said, having found Leavis's prose dense and his ideas joyless.

"Good," she said, "you'll do," and swept downstairs to her sixteenth-century literature class, obviously relieved that she did not have yet another intense faculty member to deal with.

One was obviously enough, and he was Professor Jack Vincent, a Harvard Ph.D (the only Ph.D in the English department at that time).

He was much chagrined that I had joined the department with a mere Cambridge B.A. "Life, literature, and thought," he said in our first conversation, "that's the content I understand of your Cambridge course. Skating over the whole panorama of English to find mere enjoyment. There is no intellectual vigour or discipline in that." Well, in his terms, there wasn't. No Cambridge don had ever asked me to append a list of sources at the end of any essay. But then I had read aloud every essay I had ever written to a don, one on one. If he or she doubted my sources, or my research, the thrust was sharp.

I remember Joan Bennett, resident Cambridge authority on metaphysical poetry, stopping me once while I was in full flight about John Donne. "You say in many places, Mr. Edinborough, Donne does that. Please name three."

I produced the first quickly. After a little hesitation, a second was quoted, and then I was vague.

"In other words, two examples you have actually discovered, and perhaps a third dimly discerned, is really what your argument is based on."

Years later — still, in fact — when writing a column, a report, or even a letter, I hear that penetrating, gentle voice: "Name three, Mr. Edinborough." In a forty-year career in journalism and the academic world nothing has saved me from trouble so effectively.

As for the taking of a single aspect of a poet or dramatist or novelist and, as North American universities do, building a thesis on it, my own tutor Tom Henn had once scotched that.

Writing about John Webster and trying desperately to prove something new about him, I had written a two-thousand-word essay that I confidently read to him one day while sitting on the opposite side of his gas fire in a room panelled the same year as the Great Fire demolished most of London. He listened without a word for forty minutes, then looked over his spectacles and said, "Ingenious, Edinborough, and therefore wrong."

The department welcomed me, glad that, together with Alastair Walker, I would be saving them the trouble of teaching "remedial" English. This was the coaching of those who, despite province-wide examinations, still turned up at Queen's without the capacity to write a grammatical sentence. Walker had done the same at the Canadian Staff College in Kingston during the war and, when that closed, came over to Queen's.

He and his wife were great saviours in our first six somewhat baffled months. He had been at Cambridge in the 1930s after taking his University of Toronto degree and he at least knew the same system and standards that I knew.

More than that, he introduced us to his friend Grant Macdonald, a Canadian artist who had had a gilded time in London in the 1930s. A skilled draughtsman and perceptive portrait painter, he had been the sought-after artist for the quality magazines in England, *The Tatler*, *The Sketch*, and such, doing double-page spreads of caricatures and portraits to illustrate the theatre reviews. Noël Coward, Glynis Johns, the young Laurence Olivier, and John Gielgud had all come before the public in his perceptive pen-and-wash, as well as on the stage.

His father, however, was sick, and he had, after service in the Royal Canadian Navy as a war artist, come back to Kingston to look after him. He had given up a lot. He had been in fashionable demand in London and had had two books of his sketches and paintings published, one in Canada, one in England. Now, instead of an apartment in Mayfair, he lived in a small house in Kingston where a bullying, jovial housekeeper-nurse looked after his bedridden father and him. He was lonely, and very soon we became fast friends and travelled around Kingston everywhere in his open convertible, shared with a large black-and-white English setter called Hamish.

Through him we also met Robertson and Brenda Davies. Davies, not yet a novelist, but already a playwright, was editor of the *Peterborough Examiner*, a paper owned by his father, Senator Rupert Davies, who was also the proprietor of the *Kingston Whig-Standard*.

The Davies family had been important in Kingston since 1926 when Rupert Davies, having bought the Liberal Kingston *British Whig*, had amalgamated it with the Tory *Standard*. The resulting *Whig-Standard* was Kingston's daily.

It was, however, because of our theatrical exploits that we first made friends with Grant Macdonald and the Davieses. Though we had had no connection with the professional theatre in England as they had all had, certainly at Cambridge in the Marlowe Society we had had professional exposure. The director of the plays at the Marlowe was George Rylands who, though a don at King's College and university lecturer in English, had directed John Gielgud's *Hamlet* in London's West End in 1943 and had been in New York in 1945 to direct Elizabeth Bergner in John Webster's *The Duchess of Malfi* on Broadway. ("The most excruciating experience of my life!" Rylands said when he returned to direct the Marlowe Society's *Antony and Cleopatra* that term!) And London critics always came to see and write about our productions.

Rob and Brenda were deeply involved with the Peterborough Little Theatre, and there was much hilarity when, after we had seen Rob's production of Shakespeare's *The Taming of the Shrew*, I confessed that I had had my first taste of the stage by playing the Shrew. Rob had been in the Old Vic Company in England as actor and teacher after graduating from Oxford. Brenda, his wife, had been the stage manager at the Old Vic.

From the Old Vic to Peterborough's Little Theatre was a somewhat steep decline but, as Harrison had said in his letter, "If you want theatre in Canada, you must invent it."

And so we did. We joined the Queen's Faculty Players, an amateur group that had been dormant during the war. Alastair Walker became treasurer and, having checked the contents of the cashbox, tallied all the bills and receipts, said we had some money with which to mount a show. (He found a discrepancy of a few cents in trying to balance the neglected books, which he attributed, he said, to "spontaneous lapse of coin.")

We were mainly English expatriates who came together to present Oscar Wilde's *The Importance of Being Earnest*. The director of this first show, Viola Smethurst, was the wife of the professor of classics; the butler was a professor of physics, Vic Hughes; Jack was Viola's husband; the governess, Frances Smith, was the wife of a professor of chemistry; Lady Bracknell was Kathy Roberts, married to another professor of physics. Only Dr. Chasuble and Gwendolen were played by Canadians: Dr. Chasuble by Pearson Gundy, the Queen's librarian, and Gwendolen by Margaret Shortliffe, whose husband was a professor of French and prominent in CCF circles in Kingston.

Letty played Cecily, and I played Algernon.

Did we, as some people in the university thought, do such a play as a way of soothing our homesickness? Were we wallowing in nostalgia? I don't think so. I think we did it because if we didn't do Oscar Wilde, no one else would. And he was highly amusing both to act and to watch.

There was only one professional theatre company in existence in Canada in 1948. There were only two legitimate theatre venues for travelling shows, one in Toronto, one in Montreal. Travelling shows didn't come to Kingston.

Once we saved our pennies, hitched a lift, and went to see Robert Helpmann and the Old Vic Company do *A Midsummer Night's Dream* in Montreal. The production was staged in the Forum. We sat in the reds on the centre line, our heads turned like Gulliver's Laputans. Down below us two usherettes talked all through the performance in demotic French. There were microphones hidden in the foliage of the scenery but, of course, getting near them wasn't easy for the actors and, even if it were, who wants to talk from behind a tree?

Helpmann, with his great balletic skills, did an occasional

pirouette towards them, and his voice (as Oberon) would suddenly boom out over the stands as if someone had just scored. As a moment to begin "I know a bank whereon the wild thyme blows," it was not auspicious. The smell of *pommes frites* was everywhere.

Donald Wolfit did actually come to Kingston and presented *Hamlet* at the Kingston Collegiate and Vocational Institute. But apart from his own performance and that of his wife, it was overplayed, fustian stuff. In fact, the most tragic and meaningful gesture of the whole afternoon was his solo bow at the end, clinging to the curtain still wracked by self-doubt, exhausted by his theatrics.

But the atmosphere of a school auditorium or a hockey rink was not conducive to good professional playing. In a sense, the theatre we did ourselves was more meaningful. We were part of it. We got into the text, and we quickly attracted like-minded people — not all expatriates.

The great highlight of those early days was a homemade opera. The Queen's Glee Club and the Queen's Symphony Orchestra, under the direction of the head of the music department, Graham George, were approached by two older students, Paul Roddick and Don Warren, with a libretto based on Longfellow's *Evangeline*. They asked if he would write the music for it. Graham, who had often written music for the summer school ballet students to choreograph, agreed, provided I would agree to direct it, and Letty would take charge of makeup.

Nothing emphasizes the effort required in those days to achieve a truly Canadian work more than *Evangeline*. The music was written, and the parts all copied, by Graham George himself. The orchestra was made up of students, and some townsfolk — all amateur. There was then no performance division in the Queen's music department from which to draw skilled faculty or promising students. The costumes were locally made or rented from Malabar's. The set was designed by a local artist, Martha Jamieson, and built and painted by students.

The soprano lead was Tjot George, Graham's wife, who had had some training in Holland before marriage. The tenor was a student whose rehearsals had to straddle his job at the Point Anne cement plant where he earned the money to be at Queen's. The baritone was Al Crofoot, later an early member of the Canadian Opera Company, but at this time a grade A student and massive defensive lineman for the Queen's Golden Gaels whose season was still busy when rehearsals for *Evangeline* began.

The rehearsals were held in many different places — Grant Hall, the great Queen's assembly room; the common room of the women's residence, Ban Righ; the music room; and so on. The actual production was staged at the Burgundy Room of the La Salle Hotel in Kingston, where we repaired — orchestra, cast, and crew — on Monday, November 29, 1948.

The first dress rehearsal was agonizing. Different supporting groups bickered over jurisdiction (the Faculty Wives Association was particularly difficult, my diary says baldly); the scene changes by willing but untrained stagehands who had never seen a stage before, glacially slow, the singing not always in time with the orchestra.

The next day, with 250 high school students there, it began to come together, despite the constant flashing of a *Montreal Standard* photographer.

On opening night one singer had to stop and start her aria again, and a large piece of scenery fell forward onto the stage at the end of the second act. But the reception of the piece was rapturous, with clapping and cheering, shouts of "composer," and such — as if we were premiering a Canadian *Peter Grimes*.

In a sense we were. No other Canadian had written a brand-new opera on a Canadian theme, with a Canadian score, and produced by Canadians, so it caused quite a stir. Dr. Walter, director of the Toronto Opera School, came to see, but was very supercilious. "My orchestra costs $1,000 a night," he wailed, as if by producing a competent orchestra for nothing we were somehow undermining him. John Lowe, the head of CAPAC, was there. So was a representative from Chappel, the music publishers, and John Gray, the head of the Macmillan publishing company. Reviewers came from the *Ottawa Evening Citizen*, the *Montreal Standard*, *Saturday Night* magazine and, of course, the local papers in Kingston, Belleville, and Brockville.

For all its flaws, and the *Montreal Standard* noted every one of them, it was a tremendous effort done with no subsidy of any kind, except the use of university space for rehearsal. And this was not British expatriates. All the principal players — composer, librettist, designer, orchestra members, singers, chorus — were Canadian.

But in the climate of the arts back then, *Evangeline* strutted its three performances, was nationally noted — and died. The Canadian Opera Company with its European director would not be seen near such a thing as a *Canadian* opera. So *Evangeline* lapsed into limbo, though its press notices, and the bound copy of the whole score, are monuments to what was beginning to emerge in Canada — a sense of nationality, a sense of need for indigenous arts.

But growth was hampered by the lack of any nurturing funds (the Canada Council was a decade away), by the huge size of the country (no one in Ontario, whether writer, composer, or artist, knew what was going on in other provinces), and by the still-prevalent respect for anything from "the mother country." All this, plus a national inferiority complex that puzzled me then, and puzzles me still.

Acting on my new-convert's enthusiasm, I went out to groups of people, telling them that there was talent in Canada and that they should cherish it, nurture it, and pay for it. My passionate remarks rebounded a bit when I addressed the Women's Canadian Club in Belleville. I spoke of Canadian drama, read from a couple of Robertson Davies's plays, and whipped up quite a good reaction.

"I think," Mrs. Doyle, the president, said, "we have all been stirred by what Mr. Edinborough, our new Canadian, has told us. So we should close this meeting by singing 'O Canada' with even more verve than we normally do."

The pianist clomped down on the keys, the ladies stood, and there was I, facing them all, and not a word of the piece did I know. I moved my lips bravely in what I hoped was a reasonable facsimile of the lips in front of me. But I spent an hour that night learning the national anthem.

In line with my new feelings I chose to direct three one-act plays by Robertson Davies as the next offering of the Queen's Faculty Players. They had recently been published. One or two had won awards at the Dominion Drama Festival. Davies was a well-known name in Kingston. A sure winner, I thought.

The three chosen were *The Voice of the People*, an amusing piece drawing on his newspaper experience; *Hope Deferred*, a historical piece hinging on the Catholic Church's opposition to theatre in New France; and *Overlaid*, the single most telling piece of one-act theatre ever written in Canada.

I played Count Frontenac in *Hope Deferred*, with Letty taking the lead female role, Chimene. In *Overlaid* Bill Angus, the head of drama at Queen's, played the old man with Margaret (Peg), his wife, playing the daughter, Edith.

The rehearsals went well. Rob Davies was pleased and undertook to come to the opening night in Queen's Convocation Hall. But, on the morning of that night, I got a letter:

Dear Arnold:

Woe, alas — we shall not be able to come to Kingston tomorrow. Had hoped until today that it might be managed, but no. My assistant is on holiday and our general manager (a Christian

Scientist) is in bed with a terrible hacking Error. I am alone at the helm. V. disappointed.

I enclose our tickets, tear-bedewed.

Rob

That night, a raw but not impossible February night, we had seventeen people in the audience, two fewer than we had behind the curtain. Obviously the way ahead for Canadian drama was not going to be swift, nor was it to lie among eager, clamorous audiences.

IV

TOWN, GOWN, AND MILITARY

F OR ALL THE ACTIVITY WITH which we surrounded ourselves, Kingston still seemed to us a dour Presbyterian place, aptly enough called the Limestone City. The pub, centre of a lot of undergraduate life in Cambridge, did not exist. I had scandalized a regal-looking matron early in our stay by asking her, as we stood on the steps of St. George's Cathedral after Sunday service, where the nearest pub was. When I later ventured into a "beverage room," I could understand her reaction.

There was, in fact, no casual meeting place for members of the university to meet the townspeople. Kingston, we discovered, like Caesar's Gaul, was divided into three parts: town, gown, and military. Each kept pretty much to itself.

The military was a dominant presence. There was an area headquarters, commanded by a brigadier, and a brigadier presided over the Canadian Defence College. The headquarters of the Royal Canadian Corps of Signals (RCCS) and the Royal Canadian Electrical and Mechanical Engineers (RCEME) were there. And, in 1948, to everyone's surprise, and to satisfy Brooke Claxton's wishes, the Royal Military College was reopened to train permanent force officer cadets.

I was delighted when asked if for the first year or two, until they collected the faculty together and until they were at full four-year strength of some three hundred cadets, I would consider being a special part-time lecturer in basic English, along with Alastair Walker.

G. B. Harrison, as head of the department, had no hesitation in sanctioning it. "It will doubtless help your financial situation," he said, "and it will certainly widen your social horizon."

He was right on both counts. Our financial situation was precarious. The university cheque each month was $200 before taxes. When taxes were paid, $85 went immediately in rent for a more salubrious apartment we had found nearer the university. About $15 went in monthly payments on the new furniture we had bought when we moved, leaving us under $100 for everything else.

Mind you, costs were less, as some receipts from those years show, the most amazing of which is the hospital bill for the birth of our first child, Christine Ann, in Kingston General Hospital:

Daily room service 7 days @ $6.25	*$43.75*
Clinical and pathological service	*2.00*
Medicine	*.85*
Operating or obstetrical room fee	*7.00*
Nursery care, baby	*7.50*
X ray and radium treatment	*6.00*
	$67.10
Paid in advance	*25.00*
	42.10
Discount on cash	*1.75*
	$40.35

The room cost per day then and now and how it got from one to the other is subject for a whole book, but this one is not it.

Other bills are equally eye-opening. "Five red roses," one for each year of our marriage sent to Letty on that anniversary, January 14, 1951, cost $1.70. Meat for a month for one child and two adults (all our supplies were on monthly accounts) was $18.86. The bimonthly public utilities bill was $9.53, with seventy-five cents off for payment within thirty days. Another $75.00 per month would make a lot of difference.

As to the social scene, that was quite a difference. There were regular weekly dinner-dances in the mess; there was an end-of-term ball; there was a great dinner and dance for the visit of the West Point hockey team in February; there were corn roasts; and there were sailing boats available for faculty to sail.

The white tie and tails, not worn since May Balls at Cambridge, were taken out. And the miniature medal bar, showing my active involvement in the war, only three years finished, gave me military standing.

For a young, energetic, party-going couple like ourselves, RMC was a godsend. The majority of the people on faculty, whether in the forces or civilian, were much closer to our age and a great deal closer to our outlook than most of the academics at Queen's. The cadets were a delight, too. They were more disciplined than Queen's students, but with an openness that was refreshing.

The diary again: February 9, 1949.

> *To RMC to hand back grammar tests and to have a lively discussion on what a wood nymph was. Seemed to be the opinion of one cadet that it was something like a woodchuck. But I was informed that: "Sir, he comes from the prairies."*

When the cadets heard that we had been jointly involved in amateur theatre, a delegation came to me with the permission of the commandant, Brigadier Don Agnew, to see if I would direct a play for them. What else but *Journey's End*, that First World War piece set in the trenches? It proved a great experience for them (and us), and the next year we even tried Maxwell Anderson's *Winterset.*

The circle of our lives was thus widening. I also went every Tuesday night by train to Belleville, fifty miles west down the line, to teach a small group of schoolteachers who were registered as extramural students. By taking a course in the winter, and two at summer school every year, they managed to keep a full-time teaching job and get their B.A., even if it did take five or ten years to do it. They were older, much more determined students and kept a young, still neophyte professor on his literary toes.

Leaving home at 5:45 every Tuesday, I had dinner on the train, helped by the fact that the engine stopped to take on water just outside of Belleville, giving me time to finish my coffee.

But what an engine. One of the showpiece steam locomotives of the Canadian National, it had six-foot-high driving wheels, mammoth pistons, and a wailing siren that seemed composed of all the purgatorial souls who had pioneered this country and still invested the lonely air above it. Furthermore, for an English country boy, who loved trains and had read about North America principally in juvenile Wild West fiction, the announcement as the train steamed and hissed into the station was magic: "The train now approaching platform 1 is the train for Belleville, Port Hope, Oshawa, Toronto, and points west."

Every time — even on nights when the temperature hovered around zero Fahrenheit or the snow was blowing and the wind howling and one's spirits matched the temperature — every time I heard that I felt a stir that I was now in, even part of, a huge country rolling westward for thousands of miles. What was more, this magnificent machine hissing by me could take me all the way.

Coming back at midnight, getting home at 1:30 a.m., was less romantic, although it also had its moments. On one occasion I shared the coach with a madman, who vividly and loudly described our journey as the way to hell, standing on a table and declaiming until the trainman came and, by knocking his legs from under him, also knocked the breath out of him. On another a drunk waved a revolver and kept us all on the floor until the train stopped at Napanee and police came on to deal with him. Simple enough, too. The revolver wasn't loaded; he was. But it made for an unquiet journey.

I was paid seven dollars per trip for these jaunts with expenses, including dinner, at about the same rate. (Dinner was not originally included in the offer to me, since the Extension Department thought that "most people eat before six, anyway.")

By now, with contacts in Belleville and Brockville (a similar extension course in Brockville done on Saturday afternoons — 1:15 train out, 5:00 p.m. train back), at RMC and Queen's, I had begun to be invited to address local service clubs. When I asked about what, the reply was usually the same: about anything you like for about twenty minutes. So to Kiwanis, Rotary, Lions, Civitan, Zonta, the odd Canadian Club, plus a chamber of commerce or two I went and talked about education and the shortcomings I had found in the new system I had come to.

The headline over one account of such a talk delivered to the Brockville branch of the Queen's University Alumni Association read: "Nightmare Qualities of Canada's Educational System Criticized." The article started: "University life is just one long, continuous rally, and not enough time and emphasis is being placed on cultural pursuits." The date on the piece was November 12, and doubtless the talk was evidence of faculty frustration at the slow academic start of the school year in those days.

Until the frosh had been hazed, the football team cheered, and Homecoming Week was over, no work was ever done outside the classroom. Students overwhelmed by it would ask just what they were "responsible for" this term. I remember one student coming to my office and asking, "Sir, am I responsible for 'Paradise Lost' this term?"

"Sampson," I said, "you will never be responsible for a four-line lyric. But if you mean do you have to read Book I of Milton's *Paradise Lost*, the answer is yes."

By this time my status had changed. Initially, as Principal Wallace had said, I would serve as a lecturer on a two-year probationary contract. During that time, I had started research into the Revels Office of Henry VIII, hoping to write a book that would put Shakespearean drama into a better context. I had never believed, as most of the scholars whose student I was had believed, that the Globe Theatre and Shakespeare rose like Venus out of the sea, fully equipped for its glorious time without any antecedents.

To this end I had gone to the original documents of the Revels Office, which were held in the Losely Manuscript Collection at the Folger Shakespeare Library in Washington, D.C. Three springs in a row, when term was over, I had gone for two weeks to find the documents I wanted, to have them photographed onto microfilm, and then, through the winter, spent endless hours transcribing them in my office on a machine the Douglas Library had loaned me.

What revels went forward, how they were costumed, who paid for it, who directed it, were all there in these account books. I wrote a "scholarly" article on it, which was published in the January 1951 issue of the *Shakespeare Quarterly* in the United States. When I went back to England, this would all look good on a résumé.

G. B. Harrison was interested in my project, which was very much in his own line of scholarship. Then one day on campus he said, "If you need any more help from me, you'd better ask for it soon. I am leaving to become a foundation professor of English at the University of Michigan at Ann Arbor. Come and see me in my office."

We walked over together.

"You seem to have made yourself rather popular around here," he said. "I noted recently, as did a lot of other people, that when the *Queen's Journal* (the student biweekly) announced the visit of the University of Edinburgh philosopher who will give the Dunning Trust Lectures this year, they spelled it Edinborough. You have also made your mark in the theatre and outside on the service club circuit.

"I also know that your academic work in Shakespeare and the Tudor period is being well researched and you know a lot about it. If you would like to stay at Queen's, for all its educational shortcomings," he said wryly, "I am prepared to recommend that you become an assistant professor with tenure beginning September 1. You would take over all my graduate and undergraduate courses and leave science English behind you. I assume, if your answer is yes, that you will take your M.A. this summer."

For a Canadian academic an M.A. would take longer than that. But Harrison knew that at Cambridge, two years after receiving one's B.A., a fee of five guineas would allow you to "proceed M.A.": no thesis, no lectures, nothing. Just send the money.

I knew that Jack Vincent would be furious. I knew that if Alexander became head, my way would not be so easy. I also wondered whether Letty would want to commit to Canada.

We talked about it at length, weighing the fact that, if we did want to go back, an assistant professorship, plus the Revels Office, would be more negotiable than what I now had. If we stayed, at least the pay would be better, and tenure was, if you wished, for life.

After much discussion, I "proceeded M.A.," became an assistant professor, took tenure, and committed to Canada.

V

FOLIOS
I AND II

L IFE HAD SEEMED HECTIC IN OUR FIRST two years in Canada. My twelve lectures a week inside the university, plus two two-hour sessions outside, one at Belleville and another in Brockville, kept us busy academically. *Evangeline*, *The Importance of Being Earnest*, and a public speaking club for interested students were time-consuming after the scheduled day.

We moved from Lower William Street to Aberdeen Street (Mrs. Edinborough of Aberdeen Street sent a few eyebrows up at the other end of a telephone or over a store counter). Then, with a visiting Scottish intern, we rented an enormous house on Nelson Street. Letty was kept busy with furnishing, bringing up the baby, and maintaining a house that always seemed full of students, faculty, and visitors, on a budget that, with tenure and the rank of assistant professor, was slightly less penurious — a whole $3,000 per year.

That house made us more Canadian more quickly than anything. It had a furnace that seemed forever in need of stoking. The ashes were a constant problem. One February morning I put them out for collection but noted that red-hot cinders were blowing around as I left for the university. So I put out the glow with a bucket of water. When I got back in the afternoon, the ashes, all four ash cans of them, were still there.

I quickly discovered why: they were frozen solid. I now had no more receptacles, so I put the ash and clinkers from them onto a heap in the basement, which was unfinished and capacious. I did this until the four cans thawed in late March. Then the spring rains came, the sewer backed up, and the stored ashes floated into the drain when the sewer backed down. Robertson Davies was writing *Samuel Marchbank's Diary* at this time, but even *his* furnace struggles, which were epic, did not approach mine. A whole day in Wellingtons with a large shovel finally restored order, though wet ashes spouting from a basement window caused quite a stir among the neighbours.

Teaching wholly in the Faculty of Arts was more rewarding now. The Shakespeare course was one I revelled in. I built a cardboard replica of the Globe Theatre, and it sat on the lecture room desk for every lecture. I had found that of the thirty students in the course the first year I taught it, only one had ever been to a professional theatre — and that in New York to a musical.

Since I had acted in Shakespeare at school, and semiprofessionally at Cambridge, I was determined that these students should think of Shakespeare as a dramatist, not just a poet whose language was difficult and outdated — a poet who had to be "translated" into English. They entered into the spirit of it, and I looked forward to each of the seventy-two lectures every year, given as they were on Tuesdays, Thursdays, and Saturdays at 11:00 a.m.

The other honours course I inherited from Harrison was "The Principles of Literary Criticism." All of my own experience at Cambridge in the tradition of Sir Arthur Quiller-Couch and Professor I. A. Richards was focussed here with keen young minds who brought no baggage with them from their high schools. We "analyzed" poems, we discussed symbolism and imagery, and then it suddenly dawned on me: we must do this, not with English poems, but Canadian ones.

The trouble with English poems was that they did not represent incidents that a young Canadian might know about. Take

Wordsworth's "Lines Composed a Few Miles above Tintern Abbey." Tintern Abbey is a ruin, one of the scores of noble ruins caused by Henry VIII's dissolution of the English monasteries. Every English schoolboy or girl knows that. But not only did Canadian students not know it, they did not even have ruins in such a new country.

In a sense I felt I was walking them through a museum. More than that, speech rhythms and rhymes did not transfer easily from English English to Canadian English. Says George Herbert: "I struck the board, and cried, 'No more. / I will abroad.'"

"Note," I said, "the internal rhyme."

"What rhyme?" a student asked. Then he read aloud, "I struck the board, and cried, 'No more. / I will abrahd.'"

A primrose finally persuaded me that only on Canadian poetry could I really erect my critical course.

"A primrose by a river's brim / A yellow primrose was to him, / And it was nothing more," Wordsworth says in *Peter Bell*.

I was ready to interpret Wordsworth's pantheism and build a whole session around this poem when a student asked, "Sir, what's a primrose?"

My sudden, stunned pause was lightened by his neighbour in the class. "Oh, we know, sir. Don't take any notice of him. He comes from Copper Cliff. They don't even have grass there."

What all this led to were Sunday meetings at our apartment (oh, yes, we had moved from 95 Nelson; the furnace won). One Sunday a month we had the Shakespeare group, one Sunday we had the critical theory group.

We provided rye bread and cheese and coffee. We either read a play (Shakespeare) or, what was more illuminating, read original poems by members of the critical theory group, then discussed them. All were put into the centre anonymously and drawn one at a time. Sometimes a person would find herself or himself trying to analyze or comment on his own piece. The evenings often went until well into the morning. They were much appreciated by the students for whom this sort of easy mingling of faculty and student was not then known in the department. We even mimeographed two collections of the work brought to these evenings and christened them Folio I and Folio II. I have them in front of me as I write.

These two themes of my academic life brought a widening of our acquaintance. George Duthie, an Edinburgh professor teaching at McGill, met with me to talk about *Romeo and Juliet*. He was editing it for the New Cambridge Shakespeare and wanted to talk about the staging of the balcony scene. From this beginning we grew to consult with each other more often, and through him I was introduced to the Faculty Club at McGill.

At the round table by the fireplace I met F. R. Scott, then at the height of his battle with Quebec's premier, Maurice Duplessis, and in full flood as a poet. Louis Dudek, Phyllis Webb, A. J. M. Smith (when back in Canada from Michigan), and Ralph Klein also suddenly swam into my ken. Why had I not known of them before? I asked the question of George Whalley, who had recently joined the English department at Queen's fresh from his Ph.D. in London, England.

"Because this country is so big," he replied. "Because none of us poets or faculty have money to travel. Because there is no national magazine like *Poetry Chicago*."

Whalley now shared a large office with me. A Canadian who had been a Rhodes Scholar from the Maritimes just before the war and had then served with distinction in the Royal Navy, he had gone on to do his Ph.D. before returning to Canada. He had also published a book of poetry and, like me, was as busy outside the university as in. He played the piano and organ for the Kingston Choral Society; he was commander of the reserve naval squadron in Kingston, HMCS *Cataraqui*; and he was an amusing, witty, erudite companion.

"Why then," I asked, "do we not start a magazine?"

And, in those far-off, uncomplicated days, we did.

We called it the *Cataraqui Review*, Cataraqui being the name of the Indian village west of Kingston. We asked Grant Macdonald to design the cover. George, who was a fast and accurate typist, undertook to type the whole contents. I undertook to crank the mimeograph machine from his stencils, to fold and staple the sheets, and to look after the circulation. We sent out letters to friends and for the first issue had contributions from Donald Davie, an old Cambridge friend who was then at the very beginning of his subsequently brilliant career as poet and critic; from Sir Herbert Read, whom George knew; and from Doug Lochead, Anthony Frisch, Phyllis Webb, and other young Canadians looking for a place to publish.

The first issue, some hundred copies, was sent off in May 1951. People liked it. Several took the trouble to comment on it at length. Jim Gray, from Bishop's University in Lennoxville, thought it "a fine opening issue." Lorne Pierce, of the Ryerson Press in Toronto, found it "well balanced, interesting, and a square meal. The material has distinction."

John Sutherland, whose own *Northern Review* was well established, "enjoyed reading it" and suggested collaboration between us. Archibald MacLeish wrote from Harvard saying, "It looks as though you are off to a good start."

Louis Dudek, then living in New York but about to join McGill, wrote: "Greetings and congratulations for having had the energy and inspiration to turn out the *Cataraqui Review*."

He went on to say: "I would advise you *not* to try paying for contributions. You will waste valuable funds and you will have done nothing essential to keep Canadian poetry alive. The poet cannot live by writing poetry. . . . Save your precious pennies for more and better pages of the magazine and demand that poets have a sense of dedication to their artistic craft, that they understand the many-sided importance of their work, that they be concerned with good poems as other people are concerned with rich homes and new automobiles. One does not wash one's face to be paid for it."

In full, lyrical flood he closed his lengthy letter: "What we need is contact with one another (magazines like yours) . . . you must get at the things that matter and set up a current of relations between minds. . . . The rest will follow. That the whole society (or 'culture') is so much deadwood we must take for granted; it must have been so in Chaucer's time, only he never bothered about it. We are concerned with the small group of people who understand and know one another, as the Elizabethan poets did. The rest will take care of itself; benefits will flow from it to the whole community."

Certainly we had put people into contact. Letters (and contributions) came from Earle Birney in British Columbia; James Reaney in Winnipeg; Desmond Pacey in New Brunswick; F. David Hoeniger in Ottawa; and, perhaps most significant for me, if not for the *Cataraqui Review*, from Robert Weaver, CBC Toronto.

David Thomson, the brilliant, sophisticated scientist who was dean of graduate studies at McGill, was more astringent. His letter was short and pointed:

Dear Arnold:

I seem to have walked off with your Review — *where the wild Cataraqui leaps in glory — and return it with thanks. Donald Davie's article irritated me. When he says "the poet" (English or American), I can make sense of him only by supposing that he means one poet, or a few poets, that may happen to be in his mind at the moment. So also when he says "the reader." Reaney's article is only an amusing burp.*

The second issue was put together immediately after the first. It took a long time for George to type it: he was busy writing his major critical work *The Poetic Process*. When the hundreds of sheets came to me to fold, I did it, in bed, recuperating from the flu, creasing the double page by drawing the back of a comb down each one.

I was also deep in my research into the Revels Office, spending night after night in my office flicking the films onto the microfilm screen and transcribing the crabbed Italianate court writing into readable script ready for typing. And wider scope than the *Cataraqui Review* was being offered. I had done a major article for the *Shakespeare Quarterly* on the Revels Office and had written a couple of reviews for the *Queen's Quarterly*, as well as a longish piece on Jean-Paul Sartre and the Existentialist novel. Now Bob Weaver had been in touch, and I was soon discussing scripts for CBC's *Wednesday Night* (Canada's culture night of the week in the 1950s) of which Bob was the begetter and producer.

After two issues, the *Cataraqui Review* expired, although material for a third issue — more than enough to fill it to the same standard — was in hand. There were just so many hours in the day, and George and I had run out of them.

There were other pressures, too. While my involvement in Canada was becoming exciting and invigorating, friends in England were asking when I would return. Letty was also concerned. I had found, as Harrison had said I would, keen and friendly students almost pathetically grateful for the social time they spent with us. The *Cataraqui Review* had brought many established names in the Canadian literary scene of that time into at least epistolary acquaintance. For two summers I had headed the Institute of English studies — a Queen's offering of English language and literature for Quebec francophones, which had been very successful. My research at the Folger Library in the spring and through the winter at Queen's was proving both fascinating and new.

But for Letty life was a lot of evenings on her own. The Faculty Wives Club members were older and more earnest than her old nurses' fraternity at Addenbrookes Hospital in Cambridge. At one meeting there was a discussion about how to raise funds for the organization.

"What about a ball?" asked Letty, who had founded the Cardinal's Ball in Cambridge (still a notable social event fifty years later).

"A ball?" one dean's wife asked. "And who do you think would come? Can you see us dancing — or, more bluntly, can you see our husbands dancing?"

There were now two children and, before the days of disposable diapers, they were not easy in an upstairs apartment.

The letters from England gave tantalizing glimpses of what was going on there. Douglas Eves, one of our closest friends, kept us informed of the theatre. He had been to see *The Lady's Not for Burning* and met afterwards with John Gielgud (as Douglas and I had done together after seeing him in *Crime and Punishment*). He, i.e., Gielgud, sent his best wishes and "hoped to see us again soon." The Old Vic was having a tremendous season: Hugh Hunt's *Love's Labour's Lost*, Michael Benthall's *She Stoops to Conquer*, and Michel St. Denis's *A Month in the Country*. He had also seen James Bridie's *Daphne Laureola*, a "magnificent vehicle" for Edith Evans.

A month or two later he had seen *Venus Observed*, especially commissioned from Christopher Fry by Laurence Olivier to start his season as actor-manager at the St. James's Theatre. That and T. S. Eliot's *The Cocktail Party* were both, said Douglas, "tremendous experiences in the theatre." The verbal fireworks of Fry dazzled him, but Eliot was a different matter. Under "glittering words and racy humour," there were "dark and terrifying depths . . . a level of austere spiritual striving which, precisely because it lies beneath a frivolous surface, has the real terror of the suddenly bizarre and incongruous."

What Douglas Eves did for the theatre (and he and I had jointly run the Marlowe Society for two years), Donald Davie did for the literary side. Donald, with whom I had sat my entrance exams to St. Catharine's College in 1939 and with whom I had entered St. Catharine's as the only two freshmen to read English in 1940, was still at Cambridge. Having served for three years as a naval telegraph operator onshore at Murmansk to help with the Murmansk convoys, he had learned Russian. He now stayed on, having got his first-class degree, to take a Ph.D. in comparative literature with Russian literature as his second specialty.

Divorced from the kind of bookshop that Cambridge has in abundance, I asked him to spend up to three pounds (twelve dollars) a month at Heffers or Bowes and Bowes, where I still had accounts, on poetry that he thought (a) I would like or (b) I should read. The bookshops would undertake to mail them to me. His reply was typical, being the eclectic and fastidious critic and poet he was even then: "I was quite excited, Arnold, with your commission to buy poetry for you. I always like spending money, especially other people's. . . . But is there three pounds' worth of poetry being written a month. . . . This morning, for instance, at Bowes and Bowes there was no Gascoyne or Keyes, no Bottrall, no Terence Tiller or Laurie Lee, no Vernon Watkins or Dylan Thomas." He suggested spending the amount over a longer period, but did send, that day, Rex Warner's translation of Aeschylus's *Prometheus Bound* and the selected poems of F. T. Prince. Over three years, 1949-52, he was faithful to his commission and always sent, at the same time, long, newsy letters.

He was amusing about his still being at Cambridge while his friends had gone off to earn a living.

"I now write occasionally to Eire and to Kenya, to other Cambridge intellectuals benighted like you. So I sometimes toy with the notion of myself as the Roman correspondent of proconsular friends in the barbarian provinces. But the comparison won't hold for a number of reasons, least of all at the moment when we are, as you see, in beautiful Devon, culturally more benighted than county Cork, the East African Highlands, or even the Great Lakes. Simone de Beauvoir, for instance — really, Letty, you are positively on top line. Simone is quite, quite the latest thing, and won't reach Plymouth for some time yet. . . . We, in fact, are only advanced as far as Camus, having shamefully waited for the translation of *La Peste* into English."

Other letters from people we had known less well were equally spritely, with that throwaway verbal brilliance that Cambridge had taught us both to respect and to strive for.

Were we missing something? Should I do what Peter Green, another friend, had done — go all out for writing and quit teaching? Should I go back to England to do this? Better get it settled one way or another, we thought. So, for 1952, I arranged a leave of absence from Queen's. I was given a temporary appointment as a director of studies in English at my old college, picked up a couple of travelling fellowships, and went back to England. Ostensibly I would do further original research on the Tudor Revels at the Public Record Office, the British Museum, the Cambridge University Library, and London University's Institute for Historical Research.

VI

THE SECOND
ELIZABETHAN AGE

LEAVING QUEEN'S IN 1952 WAS NOT easy. We had a staunch set
of friends. The work I was doing was exactly what I wanted
to do. I had become accustomed to the free-and-easy, informal
atmosphere of a Canadian university. What would it be like to be
back in my own college as a colleague with those who had only
recently been my mentors?

First, as always, we had to find a place to live. On my own, the
college could house me. For my family, I would have to make
housing arrangements at my own expense. An old friend came to
the rescue.

Alec Clark-Kennedy had been a great rowing man and, though
from Corpus Christi College, we had met often on the river and
in college. His father, the president of Corpus, had recently
inherited a large manor house at Great Abington, some seven
miles south of Cambridge. The former servants' wing had been
made into a ground-floor apartment, furnished. Were we interested? By return mail we took it.

When we arrived in July, it looked perfect: one big living room
with windows down to the level of the garden outside, a bathroom,
two bedrooms, one with a coke stove. We looked out onto a side
strip of garden. Our door was around the back of the main house,
next to the tack room. Over a low wall and twenty yards beyond

were the stables. A large meadow, not used by the two horses, was ours for the children to play in. We now had two; Christine had been joined by a brother, Alastair.

A bus stopped right outside the Lodge's main gates and went into Cambridge at 8:15 every morning. Alec, unmarried and living with his parents, worked in London, taking his ancient Rolls-Royce (bought from a chicken farmer who had used it to transport eggs after its life as a hearse had been ended) to Audley End every morning whence he took the East Anglian train to Liverpool Street. He would be glad of company when I started at the Public Records Office.

St. Catharine's, my old college, made me welcome. I could dine at high table two nights a week at college expense, and the Senior Combination Room was at my disposal at all times. I was, in fact, treated as a supernumerary fellow of the Society, being the acting director of studies in English.

In every way England set out to persuade us to stay. Archie Clark-Kennedy, Alec's father, had always wanted to hunt. Now, in possession of an inheritance and senior enough to control his own time (he was president of Corpus and dean of London College Hospital), he bought two hunters, hired a groom to look after them, and went off at 6:00 a.m. two mornings a week to join the Puckeridge Hunt. This was the style, I thought. As he and Wilson, the groom, went clopping down the drive, I clothed them in a halo compounded of R. S. Surtees' novels (*Jorrocks's Jaunts and Jollities*; *Mr. Sponge's Sporting Tour*) and Siegfried Sassoon's *Memoirs of a Fox-Hunting Man*.

The village had cricket and football teams, which played on a handsome field that the Clark-Kennedys of a previous generation had donated. There was a stream that separated Great Abington from Little Abington. There was a church in each (though the same parson looked after both), and every year, at the annual garden fete held on the Lodge grounds, a team from each village pulled a tug-of-war across the stream, the losers getting wet, the winners buying them each a pint to help recovery.

It was village life as it had been lived for centuries. There was the Lodge and Clark-Kennedy the squire. Little Abington had a large house, which was the seat of the marquis of Cambridge (the stream separated the two estates). Sir Fairfax-Lucy, whose ancestors had had litigation with Shakespeare, lived in a more modest house on the south side of Great Abington, and the post office was run by Mr. Jaggard, lineal descendant of the printer of Shakespeare's First Folio.

An eccentric bachelor, Mr. Crago, lived in a cottage in an orchard not far from the village centre (the pub, the post office, and the school). A rawboned, large, elderly man whose actions were as lumbering as his size, he was waiting one day for the bus with a posy of garden flowers in his hand.

"Going courting, Mr. Crago?" I asked.

"Not really," he said. "But I always thought that we treated Catherine of Aragon abominably. So every year, on the date of her death, I travel to Peterborough Cathedral to leave this on her tomb. It's not much, but it makes me, as an Englishman, feel better."

The Fairfax-Lucy family's forebears, so rumour had it, had kicked Shakespeare out of Charlecote Park for poaching. Jaggard was now looking after the mail, his family long since out of the printing business. And Crago was carrying a torch for Henry VIII's first wife. Could research for the Tudor period be done in more auspicious surroundings?

As for modern England, well, it was the second Elizabethan age. In our second summer at Abington Elizabeth II was crowned at Westminster Abbey and we, having watched the ceremony on television in the village, went up to London and stood with a million others when the newly crowned sovereign came out onto the balcony and turned on the celebratory illuminations.

England also won the Ashes, the emblem of cricket superiority over Australia, and the Sir John Hunt expedition saw Edmund Hillary, together with Tenzing Norgay, climb Mount Everest — the first humans to do so — in time to announce the fact on coronation morning.

I went back to the towpath on the River Cam and coached two college boats. We saw theatre in Cambridge and London. Old friends from the war and before came to visit us. So did some Canadians.

The Association of the Universities of the British Commonwealth met in Cambridge in 1953 for their quinquennial conference. Donald Portway, the master of St. Catharine's, said, "Edinborough, can't let your Canadian chaps go back without entertaining them. We'll give them a lunch." So a mere assistant professor found himself at a sumptuous lunch, entertaining people like Leonard Brockington, rector of Queen's; the Queen's principal, Bill Mackintosh; the vice principal, Alec Corry; plus the presidents of Manitoba, Mount Allison, Toronto, Western, British Columbia, Alberta, and all.

My university teaching consisted of tutorials — one on one. There was no doubt that these students were farther along in their first year than my Queen's students, but the gap quickly narrowed as the years went by. No question that my top honours students at Queen's could have held their own in these tutorials and the occasional group seminar.

As the year came to a close, we had had an idyllic time in many ways, but the house was perishing cold and damp in the winter. Without a car, getting back to Abington after 6:00 p.m. in the evening was impossible, unless you walked. On one notable occasion I did just that. I had been invited to a King's College Founder's Feast by Dadie Rylands, the faculty advisor of the Marlowe Society. I had been seated next to V. S. Pritchett, an almost mythical figure in modern English fiction, opposite Wilfrid Blunt, brother of the later unfortunate Anthony Blunt, keeper of the queen's pictures, and close to Rylands and Noel Annan, later to become provost of King's and eventually Lord Annan.

It was an incredible evening of good talk, superb wine, and all the attendant ceremony of a tradition dating back to the last Elizabeth's reign. I couldn't wait to tell Letty in the morning. So white tie, decorations, gown, and all, I walked home all seven miles to tell her about it hot off the table. A midnight walk through mist and silence, the trees dripping in the Madingley Woods — a walk straight out of Thomas Hardy's *The Woodlanders*.

There was a movement on Rylands's part to get me a university lectureship, but a man with a degree in music as well as literature pipped me in the final interview. And, in any case, I felt a tug back to Canada. I was not going to be made a fellow — that had always been made clear. The possibility, however, caused three high table members to call on me "officially" one night after dinner in the Hall to seek my vote *should* I become fellow. They were keen that I should endorse their choice of master at the election to be held eighteen months from then. This was C. P. Snow to the life.

If not Cambridge, then Queen's still looked good. I had tenure, I had the courses I wanted, my research could be finished there now as easily as in England, and I was already launched into a scriptwriting career for CBC. I had done a fifteen-minute programme on Christmas for Bob Weaver, which had been recorded by the BBC. I had done three scripts on the coronation, also recorded by the BBC for transmission on the CBC.

There was also a moral obligation: I had taken a Queen's travelling fellowship. They had not given it to me to defect, although Principal Mackintosh had made me easy about that in conversation at the Commonwealth gathering.

There was one problem, both in Canada and England — money. I knew that I had cobbled together a bare minimum for this Cambridge year. Now it was time to return. There was not enough left to pay fares for all four of us, nor any to cope with hotel bills while we found yet another rented house in Kingston.

My mother lent me some money. Letty's offered to take her daughter and grandchildren into her house "until, dear, you can afford to send for them." So, heavy in heart, light in pocket, full of excellent memories, and loaded with research materials, I flew the Atlantic for the first time, once again to make a new life, but this time in a land no longer new to me.

VII

A SURPRISE OFFER

K INGSTON CERTAINLY NOW seemed, even without the family, as much like home as Cambridge had. Indeed, I had laid a lot of ghosts in my year back. What several other expatriates at Queen's had found, I also had found. The top academic jobs in England were held for life, and there was only one chair in each subject. In the sixty years of the English Faculty at Cambridge up to that time, there had only been three holders of the chair, and the third had another fifteen years before he would retire.

The same was true of all the universities. Young men like myself could hope for a lectureship, which still paid peanuts (about $1,200 at the then current rate of exchange). It was possible but not entirely likely that a college would elect you a fellow after some years of teaching. But the junior fellows had to do the menial administrative jobs of the society: moral tutor, assistant bursar, librarian, chaplain, and such.

Life in the college was pleasant: a good set of rooms, meals, daily housekeeping service, typist, etc. But it did not include wife or family. My own experience taught me that. When I informed my tutor in January 1946 that I would like to come up into residence a day or two after term started since I was being married on the fourteenth and would like a short honeymoon, his answer was purely medieval: "Permission given, but you must make up the days you miss at the end of term, since marriage is not considered grave cause for absence."

Many of my friends, Donald Davie among them, lived in less convenient lodgings than even Lower William Street and, like me, they were doing extra tutorial work, extension courses, and such to make ends meet. Even Mrs. Clark-Kennedy still resented the fact that her husband had to "dine in" at least two or three evenings a week as president of his college. "I cannot tell you how many solitary boiled eggs I have eaten on Sunday nights in my life," she said one day with remarkable candour and asperity.

Kingston made things easy for me. A brand-new duplex on Queen's Crescent was available for rent when it was finished. Hans Eichner, assistant professor of German, would be happy to share the ground floor with me. Above us were to be a couple from Texas. He was a General Motors engineer overseeing the installation of the marine engines in some naval frigates then being built in the Canada Steamship Lines shipbuilding yard (the last ships ever to be built there).

The rent for two of us was easily manageable: there was space to have privacy as well as a reasonable living-dining joint space. Hans made a deal right from the start, having dined with us on several occasions. "You do the cooking, I'll do the washing-up, and we'll share a cleaning woman for housework and laundry." For a whole year I never washed a dish, and Hans never even so much as boiled an egg.

We jointly decided on what to eat, although one incident still lives vividly with me when I made a decision on my own. The man upstairs loved ice-fishing. One February day he appeared at my door and asked if I would accept a large pike he had caught. It must have weighed about ten pounds and went almost from his waist to his boots as he held it out. I thanked him, coiled it a little bit, and put it in the fridge.

Hans was out to dinner, and so was I. I came in about eleven and noted that I had a fish that seemed more comatose than dead. But I was tired and went to bed.

At 2:00 a.m. I was awakened by a scream. An ashen-faced Hans was in my bedroom, saying that there was a monster eating our food in the fridge. He had opened the door to get a glass of milk, and the pike had opened its large, wicked jaw at him.

I explained, and he went to bed, shaken. I had forgotten that fish in winter almost hibernate. So, before I stuffed and cooked the brute the next day, I actually had to kill it, which was messy and tricky in a domestic sink.

Apart from occasional alarums, not all so sensational in nature, we had a pleasant double-bachelor domestic base for the year. C. Day Lewis came to dinner with us when in Kingston for the Dunning Trust Lectures. Other visiting professors and our own friends somewhat made up for the missing family whose letters were brave rather than bouncy.

Their absence caused me to become more involved with speaking: to teachers' groups; to a couple of American groups in Watertown, New York; to a number of medical groups, since I taught freshman medical students English now and became, pro tem, a member of the medical faculty.

One faculty member in particular was a close friend — the head of surgery, Dr. Dermid Bingham. He and his wife had rather taken us under their wing. I had stayed with them when Letty had been back in England to show off the grandchildren in 1951. I had stayed with them this time until the apartment was ready. More than that, Bingham was a most successful surgeon, with a thriving and clearly rewarding practice. He drove a Bentley. He had a solid stone farmhouse just outside Kingston on the Ottawa highway. He and I did skeet shooting on his property. We went duck hunting together and had spent two or three vacations in Muskoka with his plastic surgeon friend, Dr. Ross Tilley.

His wife, Catriona, was an incredibly literate woman with a quick and sometimes wicked wit. "I may not be much of a friend," she said to me, "but I can be one hell of an enemy." Not that she was: she was so generous in her hospitality, so welcoming to all, and such an accomplished hostess, no one could possibly dislike her, even if she occasionally looked down her patrician nose at some vulgarity. I visited them often, and Dermid, while admiring my involvement in teaching, which I truly loved, seemed to suggest that maybe I should look outside the university as well as in it. As he did: running the department, being a superb teacher, but also head of surgery at Kingston General Hospital, doing a full operating list five days a week.

For the moment, though, I was happily back in the Shakespeare lecture course, spending even more time with the criticism course people, since I had time on my hands.

The Royal Military College was now fully staffed, so the special lectureship there had ceased. But the cadets invited me back to direct a performance of *Charley's Aunt*, that old chestnut of a farce that is timeless and, with effort, within the range of determined amateurs who will give enough time to it. Graham George had also been lying in wait. He was keen to do Smetana's *The Bartered Bride* as the Glee Club Symphony offering for December 1953.

"The music we can cope with," he said, "and the singers are already picked. Is it possible to stage it?"

In Grant Hall, with a single set by Martha Jamieson, *The Bartered Bride* was indeed staged on December 2, 1953, with a chorus of fifty, an enlarged orchestra, and a small tampering with the score to obviate recitative passages beyond the capacity of some singers. I wrote rhyming couplets to be spoken, which would inform the audience of the plot development. I don't remember how Graham George spliced the music.

It was a great romp and, according to the *Kingston Whig-Stan-*

dard, it was "highly entertaining" and "enthusiastically received by a capacity audience."

I spent Christmas with friends in Montreal. For four days after that I joined the Binghams at Mont Tremblant, where I am perhaps the only person ever who came *down* that famous slope in winter on the chairlift. No way, after what I had been through on the Apple Bowl, would I trust myself to ski down that appalling expanse of glistening snow.

On December 30 I left Mont Tremblant to see the New Year in with Robertson and Brenda Davies in Peterborough. It was a robustious arrival — blazing fire, Christmas decorations, presents, and enormous warmth, family warmth that I had missed so much.

We sat down to dinner, and I was lifting a spoonful of soup to my mouth, when Rob casually asked, "What would you say if my father were to offer you the editorship of the *Kingston Whig-Standard*?"

Thinking this was one of those "what if" games we had often played — the Davieses and ourselves — I looked over my spoonful and replied, "I would be so flattered and excited that I would accept."

"Well, that's out of the way then," he said. "My father has asked me to make the offer, and now that it's out in the open, and you've agreed in principle, I don't have to worry about how and when to ask you. Let's talk about it later. But first get on with the New Year celebrations."

And so we did. Having put the children into the care of Mrs. Pedak, the Davieses' remarkable nanny-housekeeper, we went off to a rowdy party at Lakefield School. The boys all being away, the masters and their wives came out to play — in fancy dress.

We blackened our faces, found gardening clothes worn, as Rob said, beyond hygiene, and went as vagabonds. I enjoyed myself hugely, but at the back of my mind I kept asking, "Editor? Why me?"

The next day, it being a holiday and Rob not having a paper to publish, we discussed the offer.

"I have never been in a newspaper office in my life," I said.

"That is what so recommends you to my father," Rob said. "You won't know that it can't be done. And knowing you, you'll do it."

"I can't type — and I don't even possess a typewriter."

"You'll write and pay someone else to type."

"And what about Canada and its politics? I've only lived here six years."

"You will bring a fresh eye to it."

I was, for all my trepidation, overwhelmed with joy at the prospect.

The next day I went to the *Peterborough Examiner*, where Rob was editor and his father the owner, and saw a newspaper being produced. In those now far-off days the newsroom was a clatter of typewriters. The ticker tape from Canadian Press rang a bell when a big national story broke. The editor, or at least Rob, went out into the composing room to oversee any corrections to his page on the actual stone where the hot metal type was locked up.

He showed me the flow of material into his office: all the editorial pages of other Ontario newspapers; a mass of public relations releases hoping for editorial support; the "boilerplate," already written editorials from the *National Geographic* and other sources.

I was daunted but committed. I had now to make the actual arrangements for a contract with Arthur Davies, Rob's older brother, who was the publisher of the *Kingston Whig-Standard*, which his father also owned.

By now Rob was a national figure, playwright, writer, and commentator whose editorials were widely read in Canada and whose book reviews for *Saturday Night* had built him a reputation as a literary critic in the United States. Arthur was well-known in the Canadian Daily Newspapers Association and Canadian Press. He was a respected member of Kingston's business community and lived in a very large house on the waterfront near Memorial Park.

Rob I knew very well; Arthur I knew not at all. I had a very strong feeling that Rob had been the motivating force behind his father's offer. Had Arthur agreed with it fully? Would he feel I was being foisted on him?

An hour with him in his office when I got back to Kingston was enough to know Arthur was as partial to the idea as Rob and his father. It was also long enough to know that here was one of the most fair-minded men you could ever hope to meet.

My salary would be that of a full professor "if that seems suitable." An increase of some sixty percent in my income seemed suitable to me, eminently suitable. I would be, in conjunction with him as publisher, responsible for the overall policy of the paper, for all editorials, and the rest of the material on the editorial page. I would have his present office, where we were talking. He would move upstairs to his father's office, a spacious and rather imposing room dominated by an almost life-size Grant Macdonald portrait of Senator Rupert Davies in his court dress as high sheriff of Montgomeryshire.

I would be expected to travel on special assignments and for business purposes. These would, of course, be paid for by the *Whig-Standard*, though no expense allowance as such was in my disposition. I would have a secretary when I was settled in a bit. His would double for me until then. The contract would begin on July 1, giving me time to finish the term and arrange for my family's return and housing. Anything I cared to write to get my hand in would be well received.

I telephoned Letty, and for once I took her breath away. "You're going to be what?" she asked.

I repeated it.

"Well, my dear, you know what you're doing. I'm sure it will be for the best. But get us over there soon so we can really talk about it."

I promised. I also promised not to tell anyone about the new job except for those, like Principal Mackintosh, who had to know.

I sought an interview with Mackintosh the next day. For all principals and presidents a request for an interview from a staff member in January meant only one thing: that he had been offered a job at a higher salary somewhere else and was coming to bargain so that he could have the raise and not the move.

Mackintosh, whom I had known as dean and had talked very freely with in Cambridge at the AUBC meetings, had my file in front of him.

"May I say first, Mr. Principal, that I have not come to bargain. I have come to resign."

"I am sorry to hear that," he said. "Very sorry. You're in line for associate professor this year."

"I've accepted the position of editor of the *Whig-Standard* as of July 1."

"Well," Mackintosh said, drawing his finger across his shining bald dome, a habit he had even when two other fingers were holding his cigarette holder, "that certainly makes the writing of a letter to the editor more attractive."

I told him about the offer, the salary, and the support I had from both Arthur (whom he knew well) and Rob, whose reputation he certainly knew and, although I had yet to talk with him, the senator.

I mentioned that we would like to keep the matter entirely under wraps for as long as we could. He agreed, within the restraint of having to find a replacement for next year. Then he wished me well, said some very complimentary things about my contribution to Queen's, and we shook hands. Next, I told Alexander I was leaving, but would not (*could* not, I emphasized) tell him where I was going.

The first flush of exhilaration over, I assessed what I was leaving behind. First my research. *The Revels of Henry VIII*, as my book was now called, was not going to be written immediately. Every mention of my absence and return in the *Queen's Journal*, the *Kingston Whig-Standard*, the hometown newspaper in Spalding, Lincolnshire, and several other places (including the CBC and many an introduction as speaker) had said that I was busy writing it. Well, all those typescripts of the Revels Office, all the hundreds of pages of notes from the Public Records Office and the College of Heralds Library would have to wait. (They still wait — still neat and ready to be used.)

Weighed against that, though, was the emerging feeling that my academic career demanded that such research be properly blessed and sanctioned in a Ph.D. programme. I had missed five years of my career during the war. There was no way I was going to sideline a growing family while we lived on research grants at, probably, an American university.

And was I a scholar in the accepted academic sense? No. Such a scholar shared my office. George Whalley was up to his academic ears in Coleridge. He was annotating the notes Coleridge wrote at length and often on the margins of the books in his library. He was editing with infinite care Coleridge's notebooks, commenting on notes in any one of four languages: Greek, Latin, Hebrew, and English.

My own talents were in popularizing, in disseminating what I knew, rather than amassing more and more knowledge on one subject. Also, I wanted to have some input into the society in which I had now chosen to live. It had been satisfying to give speeches to enthusiastic audiences and to read the accounts of them in the local paper. Would it not now be equally exciting to write these same views and know that they would be published?

To know also that they would be published in a newspaper that was keenly read in Ottawa, if only because Rupert Davies was an imposing member of the Senate.

This, then, I thought, was a heaven-sent opportunity. I would not leave my deep interest in literature; it would continue. I would not leave teaching; editorial writing was teaching in another mode. And I would not be leaving all the friends I had made. I would still be in Kingston and would still have the warmth and wit of people like Grant Macdonald, Catriona Bingham, Graham George, André Bieler, Gleb Krotkov, and others.

We kept the matter secret until March. Unfortunately I had finally told Professor Alexander where I was going. He told his wife, she told the faculty wives, and I was called by the *Toronto Telegram* on the night of March 24. Was it true, they asked, that I was going to be editor of the *Whig-Standard*? I would neither confirm nor deny, but immediately rang Arthur Davies and said that unless he made an announcement he was going to be scooped. The next day a small twenty-three-line announcement appeared as a news item in the *Whig-Standard*.

The die was cast. All I had to do now was do it, after, of course, finding a house for the family that could now come to what was finally and definitely home.

VIII

THE TRAINING
OF AN EDITOR

I FOUND US A SMALL HOUSE TO rent — a veteran's house not far from the university, and with a bus service that would get me downtown to the newspaper. It consisted of a large room — half living and half dining; a kitchen with just room for four to squeeze in for breakfast; upstairs, two bedrooms, separated by a bathroom; and a semifinished basement downstairs.

As we approached it for the first time *en famille*, Letty said, "I'm really looking forward to being shown over our new house."

"So am I," Christine, now six, said.

I took them in, walked through the main room, then upstairs, and then down a primitive kind of ladder steps to the basement.

"That's it?" Letty asked, having completed the whole tour in four minutes.

"That's it," I said, "but we also have a summer place on Garden Island where we shall live for July and August. There's a ferry that will take me into Kingston at 8:15 and back again at six in the evening."

From a professor's hours, those were very different indeed. But the small house was a house — there was no one else above or below. And Garden Island, about which more later, became the anchor home for the Edinboroughs for the next thirty-two years.

I slid into the editor's chair slowly. Arthur Davies had said he would welcome my trying my hand at editorials before the time when I would be entirely responsible for them from July 1.

So, on April 14, 1954, I wrote an editorial congratulating the Kingston Choral Society and the New Symphony Orchestra of Kingston on their performance of Haydn's *The Creation*.

COMMUNITY ACHIEVEMENT

Monday night's performance in Grant Hall of Haydn's The Creation *was an excellent beginning for two new Kingston ventures — the Kingston Choral Society and the New Symphony Orchestra of Kingston. We are unqualified to pass judgement on the finer points of their performance. We know only that the soloists were most pleasurable to listen to (especially Mr. James Milligan) and that the chorus and orchestra let their "joyful song resound" with spirit. But there were other considerations no less important in making it a memorable evening. Here, in Kingston, were no less than fifty people who were capable of singing complicated music with verve and skill. Here, also, were thirty musicians who could blend into a lively orchestra. Some of these people were professionals, some were amateurs. Many of the singers were from church choirs of all denominations in the city. The players ranged from "classical" amateurs to regular dance band professionals. Yet all were benefitting from the expert guidance and mature direction of Dr. Graham George. All were obviously enjoying the chance to work with each other, and with such fine singers as the soloists were.*

Such cooperation within the groups had received cooperation from others. It can have been no very welcome task for Queen's University maintenance staff to transform the main examination centre into a concert hall after 5:00 p.m. Even less welcome perhaps was the task of transforming it back again after the oratorio was over at about 11:00 p.m.

It seemed to us, in fact, that the debut of these two new groups Monday night was a truly community effort and the community was well represented in the large audience. The community should continue to give its wholehearted support, for if The Creation *is anything to go by, these groups are something of which Kingston will very quickly become proud.*

I reprint that editorial because it seems, as I now look back on it, that it already showed some of what I would be doing when I assumed the editorial chair fully. I would be interested in and supportive of cultural efforts in the city, about which I would know more than I did about some other things. I would use the editorial columns to talk about Kingston affairs, since that was what interested the people who read the *Whig-Standard*. And I would try to bridge the gap, no longer making much sense, between town and gown.

Two months later I wrote under my own byline three editorial page articles introducing the three plays of the second annual Shakespeare Festival at Stratford, Ontario, plus an editorial congratulating the organizers on opening night. Then, on July 1, as the last of those three appeared, I took up my office on the second floor of the *Whig-Standard* building.

The transition was shattering. I had spent all my working life in Kingston in the university. I had had an office at the top of the New Arts Building, remote from the students milling around on the three floors below. I had no telephone. If I wished to telephone someone, I walked down the corridor, past eight or so other offices to the secretary's office. If anyone telephoned me (or any other professor on that floor, and there were some twenty of us), Miss Smith walked to fetch me while the caller waited.

No one came to the office, other than Miss Smith, except at a two-hour "office hours" one day a week. It was not an ivory tower, but it was certainly sequestered and quiet.

Now I sat with two big windows overlooking Market Square, where there was an actual market on Tuesdays, Thursdays, and Saturdays. The Canadian Pacific Railway station was on the other side of city hall, which faced me across the square. Freight trains were shunted in and out of the station every afternoon, with their contents going to the shipbuilding yard or the locomotive works farther along the waterfront. As the law demanded, the great bell on top of the engine clanged all the time, since the rails weren't guarded from the public.

Inside the building the rest of my floor was given over to the classified ad department, which took orders all day and totted up the day's take on a large old-fashioned cash register that rang a bell every time it opened.

I asked Arthur, whose office this had been, whether this cash bell disturbed him. "Not at all," he said. "It's money in the till that will pay us all our salaries. It's a good sound."

I also had a telephone. What was more, it rang. People complaining about editorials. Complaining about bias in the news. People wanting an editorial to further their good works or commercial prosperity. The newsroom rang me. The composing room rang me. I felt, at the end of the day, that I had been summoned, or clobbered, by bells for eight hours straight.

We had moved over to Garden Island before I joined the paper, and even there I would sit bolt upright in my bed at 3:00 a.m. to answer a nonexistent telephone call. Letty was understanding, but the first month was really gruelling. Starting at the bottom is difficult; starting at the top is not only more difficult, you are more vulnerable.

My contract was clear. My position was editor. My duties would be "all that usually pertains to the editorship of a daily newspaper, including the writing of editorials, the carrying out of the policy of the paper as it emerged in conferences with the managing editor, and the overseeing of the general style of the reporters."

The managing editor was Robert Owen, a newspaperman all his life, well-known in the fraternity, the son of a former bishop of Toronto and brother of the provost of Trinity College. He did not know me; he knew nothing about me, and yet knew of the terms under which I had been hired.

He was tough, laconic and, under normal circumstances, not prepared to give a sucker an even break. But be it said to his everlasting credit, he never interfered with any ideas I put forward. Be it also said that I never tried to tell him, or his reporters, their job. It was a delicate, wary balance from the start, but never once did it fall into disequilibrium. We even became good friends.

His city editor was Clair Devlin, an Irishman of volatile temper, extreme ruddiness of complexion, and whose control of his reporters was firm. His remarks in the newsroom varied from caustic to devastating, but his knowledge of the workings of the city government and agencies was invaluable. Choosing my moments, I would from time to time seek his advice, always freely and often very amusingly given.

The Pense family had had a financial interest in the *Whig-Standard* before it was sold to Rupert Davies in 1926, and Fred Pense, a man well into his seventies by the time I met him, was still looking after the country correspondents. For though the *Whig-Standard* was a well-known paper and quite widely read by other editors in Ottawa, it was also, as my family gleefully used to quote at awkward moments, the leading family newspaper of Eastern Ontario.

Regular dispatches arrived on Fred Pense's desk and were published on the next turn page from the editorial and op-ed page. They came from Verona, Athens, Ompah, Delta, and Westport, not to mention Odessa and Harrowsmith.

The working rhythm of the day was soon established. When I arrived in the morning, the galley proofs of the editorials I and my associate editor had written the night before were on my desk, together with a page proof of the rest of the page and the op-ed page. I proofread all of this, and at about 10:00 a.m. went into Arthur's office to discuss them with him. His knowledge of Kingston and Kingstonians was deep and wide, his fair-mindedness was well-known, and his contacts in the newspaper world were all-embracing.

He might suggest a change in wording that would save embarrassment, or he might need to be persuaded about a particular point of view. Mostly we agreed, and any corrections were sent out on my proof copy to the composing room. Later on the senior journeyman would come from the composing room and ask me to see the corrections on the stone — that is, in the actual form ready to be matted and sent to the press.

By 11:50 the paper was locked up and rolling and I, after a quick glance at the first copy, took lunch at a little restaurant next door — Viny Morrison's. I can still smell the mingled odours of coffee on the hot plate, of short-order bacon, steak, or whatever on the grill, and the smoke from a hundred cigarettes.

After lunch, I got down to reading our paper thoroughly as well as the editorial pages of other newspapers. Then I would discuss with Mel, the associate editor, what we would write about and who would do which subject. Finally, at 5:15, Mel would bring his copy in. I would put the two lots together, put it out on the number three linotype machine, and the day would be over.

All in all, it was a very different day from one at Queen's, but I revelled in it.

Quite apart from learning the physical and technical side of my new life at the *Whig-Standard*, there was the business of learning how to be an editor. Of course, I had encouraging help. Arthur Davies was careful every morning at the reading of the galleys to point out pitfalls that I might dig for myself and the paper without my being aware. He would gently counsel moderation of some exuberant language that my newfound power might breed in me. And between us we mapped out some things we wanted to see happen in Kingston.

There was the dredging of the St. Lawrence downriver from Kingston so that the new, larger Seaway boats could come into the port and drydock as the old canallers had done.

There was the provision of a municipal swimming pool until such time as a sewage plant could be built in order to clean up the waterfront. The hospital at that time still flushed its raw sewage and waste directly into the river just out from the bathing pavilion erected in earlier days by the Richardson family, now prominent in Winnipeg. And there was the sewage plant itself to be lobbied for.

Affordable housing, then as now, was an issue that we tackled head-on with a continuing series of articles on land assembly and municipal involvement in it.

The pillars of the noble city hall had been removed when they were declared unsafe. "No mortar left between the sections," one alderman said, not knowing that stone pillars do not have cement between sections. The other councillors wanted to replace the pillars with a concrete portico. Such an affront to one of the great nineteenth-century civic buildings in Ontario prompted constant editorials, urging the replacement of the original pillars.

The approach of the La Salle Causeway Bridge was notoriously dangerous in winter. Ice formed readily on the road, which was at the bottom of a fairly steep hill. No guardrail existed, and more than one car or truck plunged into the river every winter.

These were positive, realizable editorial objectives locally. And many, I noted with pride when I went back to Kingston after 1960, had been achieved.

On the broader national and international fronts I had to pick my way carefully. I knew little about Canadian politics from the inside. The Liberal Party was in power federally, as it had been almost constantly since Confederation. The Tories ran Ontario with the same enjoyment of long-term power. Things seemed to jog along pretty well. The Constitution was the BNA Act, and no one challenged it. Some lawsuits went routinely on to Britain's Privy Council if Canada's Supreme Court verdict did not suit one of the parties involved. The Massey Commission on Arts, Letters, and Science had reported, and something was soon to be done about better funding for the arts. But there was still a whiff of the farm and parish pump in both provincial and federal politics. There were still undercurrents, historical undercurrents, that I had to discover.

Senator Rupert Davies, who owned the *Whig-Standard* and was still active in the Senate, was a constantly encouraging, constructively critical correspondent. He gave me six months of actually editing the paper before he wrote a chatty and enormously helpful letter from his home in Toronto:

> *I just wanted to say one or two things which I hope are of a constructive nature. Do not worry too much about international affairs. I know that it is difficult every day to find new subjects, and I know that many editors find the* New York Times *a source of great help. During the years which I edited the* Kingston Whig-Standard, *I did all the writing myself (with the exception of a few articles which were contributed by an old man named Klugh on such contentious subjects as "Walking Sticks," "Pipes," and other startling things). Old man Klugh was the father of Professor Klugh, of Queen's University, and quite a nice man. It was handy to have the odd filler, and while they did no good, they did not do much harm. What I started out to tell you was that I did not take the* New York Times. *It might have come to the office. I will not say that it did not. If it*

did, I never read it. In my editorial life I have never written an editorial on the Near East, the Middle East, or the Far East, for the simple reason that I don't think the majority of the readers of the Whig-Standard *give one damn about any of those countries.*

After all, we must remember that we are publishing a little provincial newspaper, of which there are twenty-five or so in the Province of Ontario. If I were you, I would do exactly what I used to do, and that is read the editorial page of every Ontario provincial daily every day. It was a "rule of the Medes and the Persians" in our office that the editorial pages of all the provincial dailies of Ontario were to be placed on my desk every day. I read them through carefully and got many ideas for editorials which I felt would be of interest to our readers, and I know many of them have deteriorated since my day, but occasionally one gives forth a bright idea. Occasionally I know it is impossible to say intelligently what one wants to say in a brief editorial. Generally speaking, however, a good half-column editorial is more likely to be read than one that is a column long. International affairs are very important, but I used to wonder whether the opinion of the Whig-Standard *in connection with them was of any great importance. Mind you, I am all in favour of the occasional informative editorial on the international situation. This probably seems contradictory, and I could explain what I mean much better if we were sitting chatting. However, I have no doubt that you will grasp the idea.*

His letters came from Ottawa, from Toronto, from Welshpool, Wales, and even from the ship that took him to the United Kingdom each year. (As high sheriff of Montgomeryshire, he spent every summer there.) His letters from Britain were always interesting on international affairs despite his remarks above. They often had wry asides that made my day. Writing from

Claridges in London in August 1955, he talked about the St.
George's Cathedral choir of Kingston, then on tour in Britain:
"We are here this weekend hearing the St. George's choir and
arranging their visit (to Welshpool) on September 1. You can tell
my son, the Presbyterian elder, that I attended two services at the
abbey today, and frankly it is not my idea of a good time."

Writing to that son, Arthur, later that year, he commented:
"Today we are enjoying a nice refreshing rain — something which
we have not had since yesterday — so you will realize how much
it is appreciated."

The senator had started life in Canada as a printer, working in
the same Brantford printshop as Thomas B. Costain, the popular
novelist of the 1940s and 50s. His eye for typos was sharp, and
several of his letters to me concerned layout, newspaper style, and
proofreading errors. The most telling such comment came from
Toronto on February 9, 1957. After a suggestion for a future
editorial, he wrote:

> *P.S. I noticed in an article on the front page of the second section
> of the* Whig-Standard *of February 5, that Peter Fleming, the
> soldier and author, was educated at "Eaton." You might spread
> the news around the office that it would be all right with me if,
> when they are again referring to Eton, they leave the* a *out.*

Senator Davies held strong opinions, some of which would not
now be fashionable. He was an unrepentant, dedicated Liberal
who, when an editorial I had written in the paper criticized the
Honourable James McCann, the minister of national revenue,
wrote me: "It is a good policy to leave damning of Liberals to the
Tory press. They will do it, never fear. I do not say that you should
refrain from just criticism where it is due, but it is not a bad idea
to temper the wind to the shorn (Liberal) lamb occasionally."

He went on to say then, and on subsequent occasions, that his name was at the top of the masthead of the paper and we should be careful not to implicate friends of his in the cabinet, remembering that they would call him up about it, not me.

Not that he ever stopped me from writing critical editorials. He did not see them until they were published.

On some but few matters I would telephone him in Ottawa or Toronto. When conscription looked as if it would come in for debate a month after I joined the *Whig-Standard*, I wrote him in Welshpool, and his letter replying was a model of fair, measured comment, ending, "I would advise you to leave conscription alone, other than a noncommittal, informative article if you feel compelled to say something. . . . Conscription is political dynamite. I would hate to be the one to set fire to it."

Over the great pipeline debate of 1956 he acted in the most principled, honourable manner one could wish for. As an uncommitted Liberal, I was both appalled at the parliamentary tactics of C. D. Howe and his pipeline cronies and apprehensive about the political fallout. As my editorials became increasingly unfavourable, the senator called me. We had a long chat over the telephone.

"Well, Arnold, you may be right, and you hold your opinions well. But the *Whig-Standard* must come to the help of the party. Please leave both columns of the editorial page open tomorrow and I will send the copy."

Which he did. And everybody knew in Kingston that it was he who had written the piece, not me.

Could a neophyte editor, less than ten years in the country, have had a more magnanimous owner? Moreover, when the 1957 election came, he wrote me to say that I had been right and he wrong. The fact that I was a new Canadian was never brought up between us. But any editorial that showed how recent my political knowledge of the country was would get a comment, sometimes quite lengthy, about the long-term perspective, full of personalities and incidents from twenty-five years of the

Liberal caucus and, even more wide-ranging, his own long life in Canada. He liked a good controversy, though, and we had a few local ones.

The musicians' union, the American Federation of Musicians, would not let the Royal Canadian Signal Corps band, which was uniformly professional and excellent, play at the opening of the Frontenac Fall Fair one year because they said it would put local musicians out of a job. Since the RCCS band lived in Kingston and the Department of National Defence was a major employer, it seemed illogical and stupid to say that the RCCS band was not full of local musicians.

When, in an editorial, I said that the Frontenac Fall Fair was being held to ransom by a few semiprofessional horn-tooters, the fat was in the fire. But Senator Davies said the editorial was "very good" when he read it in Welshpool a week later and, typically, went on to note "the word *practice* is used as a verb in the third paragraph." Giving me the benefit of the doubt and blaming it on a proofreader, he went on, "I do not mind typographical errors so much, but errors of ignorance, or what appears to be ignorance, are the bane of any editor's life. This is particularly a problem in a university town."

He also approved of an editorial written about a local Anglican parson who had blessed the colours of the Fort Henry Guard, which was made up of university students on a summer job. The Queen's football team was a notable part of it, since the constant drill in heavy broadcloth throughout the summer sent them back fit to football practice in early September.

But they were not soldiers. They took no oath of allegiance to the queen. Their "colours" were an invented thing — nothing like the colours of the Prince of Wales Own Rifles, which rested, battle-scarred, in St. George's Cathedral.

Only ten years out of the army myself, in a town full of regular soldiers, I hit out hard at the blessing of these tourist trappings.

"It was," the *Whig-Standard* said, "as blasphemous as baptizing a dolly in public."

The priest who had done the blessing — the rector of St. Mark's Barriefield — rang up in agony. He could be defrocked. I had wrecked the church's image. The bishop, the Right Reverend Kenneth Evans, rang up to chide me. Ronald Way, the director of Old Fort Henry, literally wept in my office.

But nothing drastic occurred except that there was no blessing of anything the next summer, and I grew fascinated by what Old Fort Henry in Kingston, Fort York in Toronto, and Fort George in Niagara-on-the-Lake were trying to achieve in what Ronald Way called "museums of living history." In the end it made me a strong believer in Upper Canada Village, which we supported and covered as it grew out of buildings saved from the flooding of the St. Lawrence Valley near Cardinal for the St. Lawrence Seaway.

A more personal encounter came from an editorial about the farm lobby, which still forced margarine to be sold colourless. In plastic bags each pound had a little ball of orange colour that the purchaser had to knead into the margarine before opening the package. If butter were so much different and so much better, the *Whig-Standard* argued, why did it have to be so carefully and stringently protected?

The next day I heard an altercation outside my office, and a man in overalls, Wellington boots and farm cap burst in. "Are you the one who wrote the editorial about butter?" he demanded.

"The editorials of the *Whig-Standard* are written by several people," I said, "but I take the responsibility for them all. What's on your mind?"

"I just want to know what the hell you know about farming, then."

"Apart from ploughing with a three-horse team, pleaching a hedge, or thatching a stack, I have done most things on the farm where I grew up. Why?"

His face fell a mile as he dropped into a chair. Finally he asked, all passion spent, "Then why do you write such damn silly editorials?"

We had a pleasant chat, and we ended by respecting each other's differences. A week or two later, at his invitation, I went haying with him on his Hemlock Park dairy farm a few miles outside the city.

One thing being a local editor does is to teach you a lot about human nature and the diversity of people. Like the person who called one evening to say that she did not want her name in the paper, and that the rubbish fire in her garden that had caused the fire brigade to go to it, and hence got her into the news, was "not all that big. And another thing: you spelled my name wrong. It is . . ." And she spelled it out, asking that we correct the item the next day. Obviously in for a penny, in for a pound.

There were more serious confrontations. A police constable, who was called filthy names by a young punk being obstreperous in a late-night café, pulled his nightstick, hit the troublemaker smack in the jaw, and knocked his front teeth out.

We protested. If somebody insults a person and he gets into a fight, that is one thing. If an officer of the law is yelled at in the course of doing his duty, that is another. Necessary force does not, we said, include vengeful personal violence.

The chief of police was in my office within minutes of the editorial hitting the streets at noon.

"Why did you do that?" he asked. "We'll look after the dumb son of a bitch ourselves. He'll never do it again, believe me. So why put him on view in the paper? Anyway, the kid he hit is rotten, the worst young punk we have to deal with, and we've dealt with him often! Maybe he'll learn, too."

I talked to the senator about it. Jack Truaisch, the chief, was a good friend of his.

"Oh, dear," WRD said. "Jack's a good man and he'll get over it. And you know now that you often have to fight for lofty principles on behalf of SOBs who never heard of them."

There was one editorial campaign that drew me back into the Queen's University orbit.

We saw, Arthur and I, almost simultaneously, an ad in the paper that gave notice that Queen's was applying for expropriation of several houses opposite the university library. On investigating the matter we found that the university had been trying, with somewhat unorthodox methods, to buy the houses privately and had not succeeded.

They therefore had approached the Honourable William Nickle, minister of planning and development in the provincial cabinet and member for Kingston and the Islands, for a private bill of expropriation.

The reason Queen's negotiators had not been able to buy the houses was simple: they had offered only the value of the house. But each building was a rooming house with several students. So Queen's was actually buying a business, but they were only offering the price of the property.

The owners of the houses were well-known. One was Miss Austin, an elderly eccentric whose brother had been, years before, a professor of surgery. She had after his death run a house notorious for its eccentricity, but was beloved by all who had resided in it. One other house was run by an even more elderly couple, both almost blind. The average age of the owners was well over seventy, and their main source of income was their rent from students.

A committee for the owners came into being, and we supported it to the hilt. After several days of editorializing, a meeting was arranged in the offices of Billy Nickle. Those in attendance were the university solicitor, Brigadier Ben Cunningham; the university principal, W. A. Mackintosh; Mackintosh's assistant, Alex Edmison; and Bogart Trumpour, solicitor for the house owners. Arthur and I, of course, were also there.

A compromise was reached. The university would undertake to

find alternative accommodation for the owners and provide annuities in the amount of their current rental income. They would then buy the houses at current prices. After all, the Honourable William Nickle would present the private bill for expropriation, but only on receipt of a letter from the chairman of the Queen's Board of Trustees, giving written assurance that the expropriation powers would not be used.

A year later Principal Mackintosh sent me a printed copy of his inaugural address to the Royal Society of Canada with a biblical reference. "Arnold Edinborough, with compliments, see Leviticus 25:14." Said the Bible: "And if thou sell ought unto thy neighbour, or buyest ought of thy neighbour's hand, ye shall not oppress one another."

In the middle of all this editorial activity the Royal Military College had asked me if I would teach a seminar on modern drama. It had been offered and would have been taught by Professor Peter Fisher in the 1956-57 session. But Fisher, out sailing on the lake one Sunday, had tried to run before a line squall, had broached to, and sunk, with three of the four on board being drowned, himself one of them.

By clearing Wednesday afternoon, I could manage this. Arthur Davies was happy for me to do it. He also was aware that Queen's had asked me to give a night course on public speaking once a week in the winter term.

In the fall, before either of these courses started, I was elected vice president of the Kingston Chamber of Commerce. No other person, said many old-timers, had ever been a part of all three Kingston divisions: town, gown, and military.

It was a good town, too. Through the senator's generosity we now owned our own house, a delightful English-style cottage surrounded by a white picket fence within whose confines were three mature maple trees. We now had another daughter, Sarah

Jane, and the social life the university had not provided was now sometimes too much with us.

But it was pleasant to be so integral a part of such an interesting city. We worshipped at the cathedral and had all three children baptized there. The choir, despite Senator Davies's reservations, was excellent. The New Symphony Association under Graham George was flourishing. In 1956 I became president of that organization and had the extraordinary good fortune to have Maureen Forrester, Jon Vickers, and James Milligan as soloists in Handel's *Messiah*. Done in St. George's Cathedral with the original Baroque scoring for small orchestra, it packed the place. We were not, however, allowed to charge for the performance. The dean, the Very Reverend Briarly Brown, could not countenance anyone paying for admission to the House of God.

Our silver collection amounted to approximately a dime per person. We had paid our distinguished soloists, in the first magnificent bloom of their careers, $50 for their services plus coach fare to and from Toronto. We ended with a deficit of some $300, principally because Graham George had hired some Toronto instrumentalists, noting that semiprofessional players showed their deficiencies in a small Baroque group.

That led to his resignation and my going up one side of Princess Street and down the other, dunning Kingston merchants for subscriptions. Maybe because I was editor of the only print advertising vehicle in the city, they all stumped up and the New Symphony Association was once more solvent.

It was my first personal involvement in running an arts board. The experience was seminal. It taught me that tensions between board and artistic director are always present and can sometimes mount to catastrophe. It taught me that a board member cannot ignore a deficit; he and his colleagues must raise the money through their own efforts to erase it. It also taught me that businesses don't give money to the arts; people do.

Letty was also active with the symphony. She sang with the Choral Society, but as vice president of the Women's Auxiliary of the Symphony, she helped run a secondhand clothing store, the Opportunity Shop, which made a handsome contribution to the Symphony Association's finances. She also finally got to organize a ball to which people did come (and dance), with resulting money going into the symphony kitty. (The symphony, or at least several members of it, played for the dancing.)

There was a world outside of Kingston. I followed Rupert Davies's advice and had all the Ontario editorial pages on my desk every day. Despite his advice I also subscribed to the *New York Times*, the *Christian Science Monitor*, the *Manchester Guardian Weekly*, and at least one American daily outside New York. For a month or two it was the *Cleveland Plain Dealer*, then the *Baltimore Sun*, the *Miami Herald* (to read about all the wintering Canadians) and, for a short time, the *St. Louis Post-Dispatch*.

I would sometimes write them about some misinformation concerning Canada, or ask for further details of something that might be applicable to the Canadian scene. A file shows such correspondence with the *New York Times* on several occasions; with the *Times* of London; with *Editor & Publisher*; with the NEA service out of Washington; and with many newspapers in Canada.

In the thick of things? You bet.

IX

THE OTHER CANADA

I WAS BEGINNING TO FEEL I SHOULD now go and see this country that I wrote about daily. I was also dimly aware that what seemed logical, useful, and sensible national policies in Ontario might not seem so to people living in Winnipeg and the West.

In 1955 everything fell into place to see more of my adopted country. The Aluminum Company of Canada was the biggest employer of labour in Kingston. Its works manager, Neil Hay, suggested that I should visit Alcan's megadevelopment in British Columbia, recently opened at Kitimat by the duke of Edinburgh. A firsthand account of this large-scale undertaking, he thought, would interest my readers, especially those working at Alcan. The company would put both my wife and myself up in guest quarters. All we had to do was get there.

We both had a standing invitation to stay with friends in Vancouver who wished to show us "the other Canada." Then Eric Morse, national director of the Canadian Clubs, invited me to speak at as many western clubs as I could manage. Above all, every editor of a daily paper in those days had a first-class pass on the two national railways. Furthermore, Canadian Pacific had recently installed dome cars — club cars with a second story from which it was possible to get an all-round view of the scenery through which you were travelling.

On Saturday, September 20, we embarked on the train to Toronto, my ears cocked for the announcement I had heard so often. "The train now arriving at platform 1 is the train for Belleville, Port Hope, Oshawa, and points west." It was not pulled by a hissing monster anymore; a functional diesel hauled it to us. "But," I said to Letty, "at last we are going to 'points west.'"

In Toronto we stayed with Alex and Carroll McCuaig, baby-sitters from Queen's who had now graduated and were both teaching in Toronto. They had rounded up one or two other members of their English 10 and 15 classes — people who had come and read their stuff aloud at our house on alternate Sundays. Now they were teaching and I was not. But it was gratifying to have such a party sendoff as Alex drove us down to the station to catch the Dominion Express — Toronto to Vancouver — at 11:00 p.m.

We were shown into a comfortable, quite spacious bedroom, given a thirty-two-page four-colour booklet *Westward across Canada by Canadian Pacific*, and had a nightcap in the Mural Lounge, which the booklet informed us had an original mural painted and signed by a member of the Royal Canadian Academy. We were young, we had been partying until a few minutes before boarding the train, and so we collapsed onto our bunks and slept soundly.

As happened so many times on this trip, we were awakened by the shunting of cars with all its attendant shouts, banging of buffers, and quick spinning of steel wheels. When we lifted the blind, we got a shock.

Surely we weren't in Canada anymore. We had to be on the moon. The landscape was devoid of vegetation. Black and brown rock folded desolately into the distance. There were no trees, no people, no houses. And certainly no birds sang. We were in Sudbury — Sudbury nearly half a century ago, where the smelter vapours had killed even the crabgrass and scrub brush.

A student's voice from Queen's echoed in my head as we gazed out of the window. "Don't worry, sir. He's from Copper Cliff. They don't even have grass there." He was right, but until now I had scarcely believed him.

The shunting and banging was the joining of the two sections of the Dominion (more lowly and slower sister of the Canadian), one of which was from Montreal and one from Toronto. Our car — the Lounge Sleeper — was now tail-end Charlie of a longer train that would go right to Vancouver without change.

In these despised railway days it is hard to imagine the quality of service that was offered on those transcontinental trains. Our porter made up our beds and kept the toilet facilities gleaming while we were away in the lounge or dining car. He was a mine of information about the country we passed through. He would even rouse us to see a particular sight if we asked him, day or night. The dining car was spacious, the linen gleamed, the crockery and flatware were elegant, and the coffeepots shone. The stewards wore starched white coats and shirts and were proud of their skills and dedicated to their jobs. The lounge had armchairs along the side of the coach with oceans of room in the middle so that even a tall person could really lounge. And day after day Canada glided by, visible in a panoramic 360-degree field of vision as we sat in the dome.

From Sudbury on the scenery was poor: second-growth stunted bush and scrub and endless miles of immature tree trunks. (Shades of the boat train, and was it only eight years ago?) The names of the places that were either native settlements or, more often, divisional points of the railway, were still romantic to two new Canadians: Biscotasing, Kinogama, Missanabie, Jack Fish, Chapleau. Schreiber was where Alex McCuaig came from. Some of his stories of his boyhood suddenly became believable, too. And then there was White River, often the coldest place in the CBC winter weather reports. All of these names were interpreted in the booklet, along with a brief sketch of their history.

Biscotasing — an Indian word meaning "body of water with long arms" — has "tourist camps and a district headquarters and a woods flying base of the Ontario Forestry Service. On the station lawn at Chapleau a monument commemorates Louis Hémon, author of the Canadian classic *Maria Chapdelaine*, who died there."

At 7:00 p.m. on Sunday, as we dined in luxury, we came in sight of Lake Superior. For some time we had been among the towering hills leading to it, and from now until dark we saw the primal, rocky north shore as we headed for Fort William. It was too early for full fall colour, though splashes of unimaginable red were seen from time to time, and the flaming red-gold sunset over the lake, highlighted by the dark jack pines beside us, was spectacular.

The moonscape of Sudbury at dawn, the tree-covered cliffs of Lake Superior at sunset — we were beginning to see what an incredible country we now lived in. And, as the porter said when he bid us good-night, "You ain't seen nothing yet." We had, though, finally seen what the Group of Seven had been getting at. We had seen their pictures everywhere. Now we had seen the source.

The next morning, when daylight (or the porter, who had been requested to give us a knock at the right time) awakened us, we peered out to see Telford, Manitoba. We were out of Ontario "for points west" for the first time in our lives. Nowadays it is an hour and a half out of Toronto by air; then it was two nights and a day to get there.

We had not left the train since we boarded it. After thirty-six hours, it was pleasant to get out at Winnipeg and stroll along the platform, breathing fresh air and buying a *Winnipeg Free Press*, also edited by an expatriate Englishman, Tom Kent, recently of *The Economist*, later to be a Trudeau guru.

We telephoned Ken McNaught, professor of history at United College and fellow resident on Garden Island in the summer, and confirmed arrangements to get together on our return trip. Also, at Letty's insistence, we called Elizabeth Edinborough in Regina, telling her when the Dominion would arrive there and asking if she would meet us for the station stop.

Elizabeth was the widow of my father's youngest brother, who had come out to Canada in the early 1900s. He had worked in Ontario, married Elizabeth, who came from Ottawa, and then homesteaded in Rosetown, Saskatchewan, sending us the growing pictures of his family. Like my father, he had been a farm labourer. He thought cheap land on the prairie was an easier way to become a farmer than my father's, who had done it by renting land until he had saved enough to buy it.

But Saskatchewan prairie wool — the matted roots of prairie grass — was not the friable loam of Lincolnshire. And the Saskatchewan prairie was not the sociable place the Ontario countryside was. One winter sent Uncle Harry scurrying to Regina, where he got work building the new street railway. When it was built, he had an even better idea. He got a job as a tram driver — inside and warm.

Seniority caught up with him, though, and towards the end of his working life he was promoted to inspector and found himself back outside checking the timetable of the trams as they rattled warmly past. He had died a year or two before while still working. I had never met him, nor his wife, but we had corresponded and sent Christmas cards now that we were in Canada.

"You cannot possibly stop in Regina for half an hour and not meet her," Letty said. "That's what everybody does."

She was right. The platform at Winnipeg was full of people visiting with family and friends while the train crew changed and CP generally renewed itself for the next leg of the journey. We had arrived on time in Winnipeg at 8:50 a.m. We were to leave at ten. In Regina we would arrive at 6:05 p.m. and leave at 6:25.

With a warm feeling that we would meet relatives later in the day, we boarded again. No one but an immigrant can know that feeling of seeing one's own in the new country. Just as the trip so far had given us powerful visible confirmation of what we had so far known of Canada from books or paintings, we felt even more a part of it now that we were going to see blood members of our own family in the middle of this vast land.

All afternoon I looked at the prairie landscape, trying to see what the booklet promised us: gophers and coyotes, as well as hawks and "Breevers blackbirds." For the latter, the author did have the good sense to say we would have to have "sharp eyes." Sharp eyes indeed to see a bird two-thirds the size of a grackle and differentiated from it only by having "a white-eye," according to Roger Tory Peterson's *Field Guide to the Birds*.

Just after 6:00 p.m., as promised in the timetable, we rolled into Regina's train station. We did not know Aunt Elizabeth, but I had a beard and she had seen me on television from time to time. She also knew we were on the last coach. We stepped down almost into her arms.

Cousin Gilbert was with her. We chatted about my father's operation from which he was recovering, and about her other son Leslie, who had visited my parents in England during the war when he was serving with the RCAF. We talked of the trip and were sorry that we were coming back via Saskatoon on Canadian National, and so would not see them again.

Then it was "All aboard," the bell clanged on the engine, and away we went. It had been an emotional meeting, not out-wardly — Aunt Elizabeth and Gilbert were too prairie-prim for that — but inwardly. We had discussed family matters with family members in a land that so far knew us only as individual newcom-ers with no roots and certainly no branches. In a sense the short Regina stop had changed that.

We celebrated with a dinner not known on airlines or trains for many years now: homemade soup, succulent prairie beef, fresh vegetables picked up in Winnipeg in the morning (we had had Winnipeg goldeye for lunch), dessert, cheese, and a half bottle of very drinkable red wine.

We moved from the dining car to the dome, sat, just the two of us, and watched the line stretch out in front of us into infinity, seeing the signal lights change from green to red then back to green, listening to the wail of the siren as we streaked through places like Grand Coulee, Antelope, Gull Lake, Piapot, and Maple Creek, at which point, since it was midnight, we went slowly, still hand in hand, down to bed.

We were awakened by the bang of buffers as our dome car was once more shunted around in Calgary, making up the smaller train that would go on to Vancouver. It was only 7:30 a.m., but we got up and made the restaurant car just as the trainman came in to have his breakfast. We asked him to join us, the only three people in the place.

"The usual?" the steward asked him.

"Yep," he said. "After all that shunting around, I got quite an appetite. A good western breakfast will put it right."

"I'll have it, too, then," I said, though Letty settled for bacon and one egg.

"A good western breakfast" started with hot porridge, cooled with cream and brown sugar. Next came a medium-rare steak with two fried eggs on top and surrounded by crisp hash browns. Hot coffee, constantly replenished, washed it down, with buttered toast and marmalade to top it all off.

"My God," Letty said, "you'll burst." But I didn't.

We were now in the very heart of the Rockies. How many times as a boy had I heard and sung "When It's Springtime in the Rockies"? Now I was actually here, not in the springtime, but in glorious fall sunshine.

For a person born in the flatlands of England's eastern counties, and who had lived all his working life in the equally flat countryside of the St. Lawrence Valley, the first sight of Banff and its surrounding mountains was magical. We knew mountains, of course. We had spent a deferred honeymoon nine years before in Crans-sur-Sierre, Switzerland. I had walked all through the Abruzzi mountains during the Italian campaign as a forward observation officer for the artillery regiment supporting the Twenty-fourth Guards Brigade. But these mountains went on for miles, and hours, culminating in the Spiral Tunnels where we could actually see the spiral effect on our long train.

The place that hit with a bang, however, was not the Yoho tunnels. It was Craigellachie, an insignificant spot except for being the place where the Canadian Pacific had become a through railway. We had reached the site of the last spike that had joined the tracks coming from the West Coast to those coming from the East on November 7, 1885, almost exactly eighty years before.

I had been expecting the place, since I was reading the second volume of *The Old Chieftain*, Donald Creighton's superb biography of Sir John A. Macdonald. Not only were we riding through the whole Canadian landscape, we were, as an American friend had said at Cambridge years earlier, "sure riding on history."

All day long the forest gloomed, the mountains shone, and even the wildlife cooperated. We saw elk and deer and mountain sheep, but no bear. Dusk fell at Sicamous, and we had our last dinner of the trip.

We arrived in Vancouver at 8:15 a.m., breakfasted and ready to greet our Vancouver friends who were waiting for us on the platform.

No present-day Canadian, new or native-born, can do that trip. Yet nothing could so impressively illustrate Canada's history, topography, and identity. It was the trip of a lifetime and is now itself history. The more's the pity.

For an expatriate Englishman, going to Vancouver is like going home. The lawns were lush green; we had left ours a rather tired yellowy-brown after a scorching summer. The flowers growing in the gardens were the kind that flourish in England, but can't survive Ontario's winters. There were tall hedges, even clipped into topiary shapes. There were bookstores, secondhand and new. We had only one bookstore of any kind in Kingston, run by a man who had desperately wanted a B.A. in literature at Queen's but had not made it. There was a damp coziness about Vancouver that grabbed us from the start.

What we did not have were mountains. For the whole of our two-week stay the mist and low clouds never lifted from Grouse Mountain or the farther off coastal range. We did have the university to explore, and we dined in Chinatown, a Chinese graduate student as our knowledgeable guide. We met people we had known in university circles. And we renewed our acquaintance with John and Pat Chapman and Ron Baker, our fellow passengers on the *Aquitania*.

Then we set off on another adventure, once again to broaden our Canadian horizons. We left on the airport bus at 6:00 a.m. one drizzly morning to get the plane to Kitimat. Arriving at seven, we were told at 7:30 that our plane was out of service but that the mechanics were working on it. Time went by, and a young woman with a baby became more and more anxious. "Maybe we won't get in today at all," she said. We pooh-poohed the idea. Trains and planes always left when they said they would. We had not then travelled far in the frontier country of Canada.

By noon the plane was ready we were told. So we shouldered our bags and walked out onto the tarmac. Letty had never flown before, and I had only done the one transatlantic trip.

"Is this it?" she asked as we walked towards a Pan American Clipper just in from Tokyo.

"No, dear."

"That must be it then," she said, pointing to a DC-3.

"No. It's the one parked partly under the wing of the DC-3."

She stared somewhat dazedly at the Grumman Mallard — workhorse of the fledgling Pacific Western Airlines fleet. When we boarded up the retractable stairs, Letty asked a man in brown overalls, "Is there a stewardess?"

"Lady, there isn't even a john on this plane. Welcome aboard, though. I'm your pilot."

So he was, and a good pilot, too, because he flew in and out of the coastline well below the mountains. The trip was choppy, sometimes downright bumpy, and often just below ugly dark blue clouds.

"Tighten your belts, folks," the overalled pilot said. "We're here."

We whooshed lower straight towards a forested cliff, and suddenly a wall of water engulfed us on each side. We've crashed, I thought. But we hadn't. The Mallard took off on wheels at Vancouver, but landed on pontoons in Kitimat, then wheeled slowly up the shingle beach to a hut that served as the airport.

We were met by Stan Rough, the director of the Kitimat Recreation Hall, chief organizer of tours in Kitimat for visitors and of fun and games for the residents. I could not believe that middle-class, middle-brow Canadian culture could so quickly be imposed on a frontier town composed almost exclusively of Portuguese, German, and other immigrants.

Neighbourhood A was the only one built at that point on the townsite, but already there were eight different church denominations with priests and pastors on-site. There were ads in the *Kitimat Northern Sentinel* for night school courses. There were separate hobby clubs for art, bridge, photography, chess, drama, Scottish dance, square dance, and music (the Kitimat Little Symphony yet). For sports there were curling, basketball, bowling, floor hockey, skiing, tennis, and sailing. And there was a home and school association, a community chest, a Canadian Legion, an Elks Lodge, a Masonic Lodge, and the Order of Royal Purple.

All of these groups met in and around the vast recreation hall, the next largest building on-site to the beer hall. Stan Rough was a dogged man. He had been instrumental in generating all this activity, and he certainly wanted to tell us about it.

The roads were muddy, the houses rawly new in the landscape, but the Canadian way soon knocked any frontier spirit out of a company town. The smelter, which spawned all of this activity, was just coming into production, with only two potlines working. Like any other molten metal operation, it was both menacing and fascinating to any lay person who could not believe that men could work in such grubby, dangerous, and searingly hot conditions.

The staff house and visitors' accommodations were very upscale. The company in the evening was well dressed and sociable. You could take those Montreal executives' wives out of Westmount, but you could not take the Westmount out of the wives. More power to them, for this was rough living, despite the comfortable houses and superb chef in the visitors' kitchen.

Yip Radley, our host and the man in charge of the whole Kitimat-Kemano operation, had arrived at the spot by helicopter. They had cut down trees for the first supply depot. Workers to build the smelter had been housed in an old Mississippi riverboat barge up the coast and moored opposite.

They had then proceeded to dam the Nechako River flowing out of Tweedsmuir National Park, sending its waters roaring down a ten-mile tunnel through the mountains to a powerhouse at Kemano. The fall in the tunnel was sixteen times the fall at Niagara. The power created was then carried by high-tension wires over fifty miles of mountain and glacier to Kitimat. The scheme was so vast in scope, so daring in execution, and so swift to completion that we were flabbergasted, even more so when we flew to Kemano in a four-seater Grumman Widgeon the next day. I sat in the only seat available to me — the copilot's. "Welcome aboard," the pilot greeted me. "Sit here, but for Christ's sake, don't touch anything."

Letty sat with the other two passengers: one a salesman in grinding wheels, the other in soldering equipment (big items in building a ten-mile, metal-lined tunnel).

Kemano was awe-inspiring both in its site and how it had been achieved. There was no land at sea level to build the powerhouse, so Alcan had hollowed out a cave 80 feet wide, 135 feet high, and 700 feet long. St. Paul's Cathedral could sit in it and be dwarfed. There would even be room for St. Peter's in Rome, as well.

The rock thus quarried out was dumped into the water and became the townsite — was, in fact, still becoming the townsite. There were a few cars about.

"Why?" I asked.

"Well, some of the men feel if they can drive out along the road to the landing stage, they are not quite so isolated," I was told.

"How long is the road?"

"Oh, about a mile and a half."

"That's it?"

"That's it."

After a breathtaking tour of the powerhouse, we adjourned to our comfortable guest quarters, had a shower, and changed into more seemly garments for dinner.

As well we did. Rufus Rumfeld, the site manager, had a stunning wife who now appeared in basic black with pearls. Our visit was cause for celebration, and celebrate we did, not only the occasion, but the achievement. Accomplished in three years, Kemano was the new, forward-looking side of Canada, the modern and lineal descendant of the railwaymen who had built the Yoho tunnels and pushed two separate rail systems through the Rockies, the Selkirks, and the Coast Mountains.

The project was pioneer and yet quickly patterned, savage (grizzly bears were a problem at the Kemano dump), awesome, and yet already set in the same civic rhythm as old established Kingston. And there were some elements of frontier camaraderie and innovation.

Flying back from Kemano, the plane suddenly banked, preparing to land in a small lake.

"Old Bill's day off today," the pilot said. "I have to pick him up and take him out."

Old Bill (who was not, when we finally drew up to him, all that old) was solitarily in charge of the way station on the transmission line. Once a week he hitched a lift with the daily Kitimat-Kemano plane. Because there were already four on board, he had to scrunch up at the very rear of the cabin, thus weighing down the tail and helping us to get airborne again. We missed the main trunks of the great pines ahead of us, but the pontoons swished noisily through the topmost feathery branches.

We had been where few Canadians had gone. We had seen what was a world-stirring project with our own eyes.

The *Illustrated London News* had given it huge, five-page coverage in the March 12, 1955 issue, and the *Architectural Forum* had devoted thirty-two glowing pages to it — Kitimat, first complete new town in North America — in October 1954.

We felt exhilarated, knowledgeable, and thankful for the opportunity to see it, as well as so much of Canada, as we boarded the Canadian National's Super Continental for our return journey, which would be broken at Edmonton, for Red Deer, then at Saskatoon, for Prince Albert, and finally Winnipeg before we returned to Kingston and the *Whig-Standard* in October.

X

PASSIONATE CONVICTIONS

THE TRIP BACK THROUGH THE ROCKIES on the Canadian National's Super Continental was not as spectacular as the CP western route, and the CN did not then have the dome cars. But it was on this return trip that I became a national Canadian Clubs speaker.

Television was still new, and distances were not as yet annihilated by jet airplanes. So the Canadian Clubs existed as one of the places where visiting speakers of national standing, either through their positions or their capacity as communicators, could be heard. They did this on a cross-country tour, their itinerary and subjects arranged by the national office in Ottawa. The whole purpose, paralleling that of the CBC (and, indeed, the railways in the previous century), was to give a sense of belonging, of unity, and of cohesiveness.

The national director was Eric Morse, a man whose passion was Canada. He travelled across the country constantly, galvanizing the less well-organized clubs into more productive activity, encouraging the smaller ones to accept less prominent speakers. He had a network of listeners to feed him tips on speakers they had heard who should be on the national circuit. He was, typically and symbolically enough, an ardent canoeist, and long before Pierre Elliott Trudeau made it fashionable, Eric Morse had paddled the great northern rivers and published an expert guide on the fur trade routes of three centuries before.

I had spoken to the clubs in the Eastern Ontario area: Brockville, Belleville, Cornwall, and Ottawa, and had been written about with enthusiasm to Eric, who had himself heard me in Ottawa.

Mostly at this time it was on educational matters that I was speaking in Ontario. Eric quietly discouraged me from doing that in the West and elsewhere.

"Education is a provincial matter," he said. "It is also at the present time a controversial local matter. Canadian Clubs look for information, not hobbyhorses."

My topic for this national speaker's debut was Canada in a divided world. The speech reads like a chapter out of history: McCarthyism in the United States; the Cold War in Europe; the question of mounting agricultural surpluses in the developed nations; the constant undernourishment of the Third World; and the spectre of famine. It argued forcibly, or at any rate, as forcibly as I felt a Canadian Club speaker should, for a more outward-looking Canadian foreign policy and a concentration on sharing the world's wealth rather than putting huge sums of money into armaments to keep the favoured nations safe.

Our friends in Edmonton lent us their car to drive to Red Deer, which we found in early October to be dusty, without much character and, after Vancouver, small.

It was an evening meeting, and the president of the club took us to dinner at a place that reminded us strongly of the United Cigar store we had, some years before, breakfasted at in Kingston. The talk was pleasant, though, and both Letty and I were feeling pampered by the time we got to the school where the meeting was to be held.

There was an impressive turnout. The chairman was pleased at it, especially since this was the opener for the year where season subscriptions were sold. He asked, after we had saved the queen, whether he could transact a little business first before calling on me. This was usual, so I agreed.

"Now, ladies and gentlemen," he said, "as you can see, a lot of people have turned out for this first meeting of the Red Deer Canadian Club. In fact, I am told we have over 350 people in the audience, which is more than we have ever had before. It says a lot for the efforts of your board who have really done a job in selling tickets. I want to say thank you to them all. But keep it up. We need at least 500 people every meeting if we are to get the calibre of speaker that we really want. Tonight our speaker is . . ."

Letty, sitting in the front row, burst out laughing. The rest of the audience took their cue from her. I joined in the merriment.

A very red-faced chairman then struggled with the introduction and soon left the dais to me. Obviously Canadian Club speaking would have its surprises.

Later, and farther east in Saskatoon, I learned another valuable lesson. I had opened my speech in Red Deer with a golfing story which, by innuendo, linked two men with each other's wives. Red Deer had thought it hugely entertaining and a little racy, but not enough to shock a mixed Alberta audience. In the Bessborough Hotel in Saskatoon the women's Canadian Club sat absolutely silent at the punch line. Those that did get it did not want those who didn't (a majority obviously) to know that they did. Later, the people at a supper meeting in Prince Albert also enjoyed the story.

I had been learning fast about the variety of Canada from our rail and air travels. Now I began learning about the variety of Canadians.

All three clubs gave favourable reports back to Ottawa, and so began a love affair between myself and Canadian Clubs, a relationship that was further developed because of another factor that now entered the equation: crime comics and obscene literature.

The parents of the baby boom were a new breed of involved people. They questioned the education system (which had led to my talking about that so much outside of Canadian Clubs). They were appalled at the violent crime comics they found in their kids' possession. A trip to the local variety store showed them the emerging "adult" magazines led by *Playboy*. To a Depression generation that had come through a war, this sort of explicit material was unknown. Women with bare breasts had been an occasional (for a boy, anyway) lucky break in the *National Geographic*. But here were page after page of young nubile bare-breasted women in the astonishingly true new four-colour printing process.

The Catholic Women's League took up the cause, and the provincial government was forced to take note, as well as the federal department of justice. Ontario, therefore, appointed a Committee on Salacious Literature. Chaired by the deputy attorney general, William Common, and put together by his minister, the Honourable Kelso Roberts, it had to be seen to be balanced — not all Catholic Women's Leaguers — and to be geographically representative. As a former professor of English literature, a speaker on educational matters, both in Ontario and on the CBC and, most important, *not* from Toronto, I fitted the committee's selection guidelines and found myself a member.

The committee consisted of four men: John Elliot, the associate editor of the *London Free Press*; a parks department employee from the Lakehead; Bill Common as chairman; and myself. The four women were all Catholic Women's Leaguers: one each from Toronto, Sarnia, Windsor, and Ottawa. We met at the legislative buildings. Our discussions were friendly, circumspect, and did what all such committees do — played for time for the government that appoints them.

In the end we formed a consulting board to which people could send material they found objectionable. That board could then suggest, if they found the feeling justified, to the magazine wholesalers that certain titles might run into trouble from the morality squad of the Ontario Provincial Police. It was discreet, quiet, backstairs censorship. But the wholesalers were happy to cooperate. Court cases were expensive, time-consuming, and usually not worth fighting. But who as a wholesaler, member of his local chamber of commerce, perhaps a Little League hockey coach, wanted it reported that he was guilty of offering obscene literature for sale?

It was an eminently sound political solution to the immediate problem. But it did not address the vital parts of the matter: the question of censorship and the matter of community standards by which the law found such material guilty or not guilty.

I suggested, since this was a vital national issue, that I might address Canadian Clubs on the subject. I suddenly had a tiger by the tail. Everybody wanted the topic (even Red Deer). In the 1957-58 season I spoke at Charlottetown, Prince Edward Island; Moncton, St. Stephen, and St. Andrews in New Brunswick; Hamilton, London, Kitchener, Brantford, Sarnia, Chatham, and St. Thomas in Ontario; and Shawinigan Falls and Saguenay in Quebec. I even spoke in Montreal and Toronto.

This was seeing Canada firsthand. The accommodations varied. In St. Stephen and St. Andrews, said my report to Eric Morse, "the accommodation in tourist homes may be the only thing that the two places have to offer, but I found it a little fatiguing to have to make conversation during lunch in St. Stephen to a relatively uncommunicative family after travelling four hours by bus."

I should add that bus and train were the major ways of getting to places: rental cars were still not widely offered, nor widely used.

"In St. Andrews," I went on, "the tourist home apparently had six boarders for the winter, and so when I wanted to leave early, it took me exactly one half hour to get into the one bathroom and I had to keep the man who had offered to give me a lift waiting for twenty minutes."

In Charlottetown the Canadian Club was a prestige affair. I was shown into a magnificent suite at the Charlottetown Hotel by my guide, Mr. Justice Tweedie. After my talk that evening, he said, "We didn't know whether you would drink rye or Scotch as a nightcap, so we provided both." He then called for silence in the crowded sitting room, said that we had all had a good evening and that the speaker would now like to go to bed. Everyone scuttled off, and when I went through into the bedroom, there was a bottle of Chivas Regal and a bottle of Crown Royal, one glass, water, soda, and ice.

Tweedie was a jokester. That morning he had showed me around the town and suddenly said, "You don't have a handkerchief in your top pocket. I think you should for coffee with the lieutenant governor."

He took me into a gents furnishings store where a very courteous salesman supplied me with a handkerchief for which he would not let me pay. "You are a guest here, sir," the man insisted.

So off we went at 11:00 a.m. to the handsome residence of the lieutenant governor and, as we were ushered into the drawing room, there was my salesman. His Honour T. W. L. Prowse's family owned the men's quality shop.

Canadian Club speakers were a varied lot. But we were never as varied as our listeners. I have vivid memories over the years, nearly all of them happy, and spread over many return visits to the same places: Charlottetown, Edmonton, Victoria, St. Andrews, Arvida, La Tuque, the Eastern Townships, northern Vancouver Island, and even with the armed forces at Baden-Baden and Lahr.

The deal was always the same: twenty-five-dollar honorarium, first-class tickets by rail, best accommodations possible, and people to meet you and see you off.

How else would I have met with the Prince Edward Islander who pointed out that they kept their lieutenant governor in a mansion while Ontario provided no house with the job? "It's not money, you see, Mr. Edinborough. It's pride. We have it. They don't."

Or the two elderly ladies who ran a small hotel in Memphracook and opened it specially for me when I next went to New Brunswick, carrying my cases nimbly upstairs, even though I was half their age and twice their build.

There was the retired colonel who took me aside, also in New Brunswick, and said, "Get rid of these people and come home for a nightcap." We did, and he drove me for half an hour to a Charles Addams-type house where we slowly killed almost a bottle of Scotch, soaked up with the most delicious medium-rare cold venison sandwiches, homemade chutney and homemade bread.

And the woman in St. Stephen-Milltown who asked me how I could possibly be on the CBC when they broadcast such obscene plays (this was Andrew Allen's notable "stage" series). I can see her withered dewlaps quivering with indignation even now.

No wonder I still think New Brunswick has more eccentrics per thousand than any other place in Canada.

Reading, too. Sometimes I would have two days in one place, or even a weekend. I remember on two howling, blizzardy days being snowed in at Arvida. In my comfortable, thick-walled, cozy room I read almost half of the New English Bible's Old Testament, ready to review it later. In Charlottetown one beautiful fall weekend I read the whole of the second volume of Randolph Churchill's biography of his father. In Fredericton I read the whole of the biography of Field Marshall Lord Alanbrooke.

That all this took place in the Maritimes told me something else: the Maritimes communications network was not like that in the rest of Canada. In Southwestern Ontario I did four speeches in three days and was back in Kingston on the fourth morning. In the Maritimes, getting from Saint John to Fredericton, then to Charlottetown, meant a lot of waiting for the one train or plane of the day.

For fifteen years, from 1955 to 1970, either as editor of the *Kingston Whig-Standard* or *Saturday Night*, I spoke to Canadian Clubs from Comox-Port Alberni in the West to Charlottetown and St. Stephen in the East, to clubs of some fifty or sixty people in Morrisburg, Ontario, to the huge women's clubs in Ottawa, Toronto, and Victoria.

I loved it, and I loved them. No immigrant to Canada ever met so many different people in so many places on such a personal level.

It was not, however, because of my speaking about censorship, but my speaking on education, that brought me to the attention of the country at large.

We had by this time two children in school and I had therefore a close-up view of the beginning of the education system and, having taught for seven years at Queen's, a very close view of its postsecondary product. Neither views were encouraging to a parent or employer.

On November 13 (fateful day) I addressed the Ontario Association for Curriculum Development in a packed ballroom in Toronto's King Edward Hotel. The OACD was a powerful group of parents, educators, trustees, and others who were disturbed at the seeming incapacity of the system to cope with modern education. Remember that this was the time of *Why Johnny Can't Read*, a disturbingly blunt book written in the United States but applicable to Canada. It was the time when provincial governments had been seen to be confused and overwhelmed by the numbers of children they had to develop a system for. Despite the facts of the baby boom, which were well-known, when the baby-boomers got to the age of six, there was a crash building programme to cope. It was happening again in 1955-56. The kids had been in elementary school for eight years; now there was a panic because there were not enough secondary schools built. (It would happen again five years later: there would not be enough universities, either.)

Teachers felt all these pressures more than most since there were not going to be enough teachers, either. A high school principal in 1956 told a meeting that he was in Toronto looking for teachers to go to his school at the Lakehead. "I need bodies in the classroom," he said. "I just hope I can find warm ones."

My concern was with the core subjects. Dick, Jane, and Spot — those egregious characters who had replaced the prewar readers with pablum instead of challenge — were not awakening any wonder in any child. At their most impressionable and imaginative age children were being processed through a graded vocabulary by rote. They got turned off, and the next ten years of school were a drag for them and their teachers.

With the passionate conviction that I was right, I tore into the education system that evening, egged on by a crowd who agreed. I quoted Stephen Leacock, showing that this year's crisis was not without precedent.

"Our studies have drifted away from the single-minded absorption of learning. Our students today live in a whirl and clutter of student activities. . . . Life is a continuous rally, a rah-rah . . ."

This crowding of the curriculum with driver education, sex education, the running of school yearbooks, and so on I blamed on the American influence of the graduate schools of education in that country: Columbia Teachers' College and Chicago's School of Education.

In a passage that made me blush the next morning when I read it in the *Globe and Mail* report of my speech, I really poured it on: "We are so concerned with outside happenings that we forget the horse inside, which is a stolid Canadian workhorse, not a semi-sophisticated, bean-fed American stallion pecking its oats of manifest destiny."

Still harping on the American way, as expressed in its egalitarian theories, I went on: "By trying to make everyone equal, we are denying the right of equality of opportunity, which is more important."

I concluded: "Finally we must make our children work harder. We have lost the idle rich, but we seem to be training a race of idle poor."

There was a standing ovation. Any scoring off the Americans and establishing our own moral and educational superiority would always hit a responsive chord. As a new Canadian, I was getting that right.

When the meeting was over, the minister of education, a tired old party hack, W. J. Dunlop, came up to me and said over an open microphone, "Well, my boy, you'll grow up one day."

Without thinking, and stung by his condescension, I answered, "Yes, Mr. Minister, and *I* have time on my side."

It was rude, it was heard, and the exchange went ringing around educational circles for some time. In a sense, I suppose, it was still there when Dunlop and I had a proper go at each other in Sudbury six months later.

I had been invited to address the Sudbury district of the Ontario Secondary School Teachers' Federation. Secondary school teachers were even more twitchy about the lack of proper planning for the influx they knew they would face within two years. Having done some research, I came out with both barrels blazing. "Three out of every four science specialists in Ontario secondary schools will be retired within the next five years," I pointed out, "yet within that same period fifty thousand more pupils will apply for science courses throughout the province."

By my calculations, I noted, there would have to be ninety-eight hundred new teacher appointments in the secondary school system if the teacher-student ratio were to remain constant.

"No one has the least idea where these teachers will come from, least of all the minister of education, W. J. Dunlop, whose Ontario College of Education cannot supply a quarter of what is needed."

Dunlop was in Sudbury to address the conference the next day. He denied my statements, dismissed the figures, and then said, "My friend, Mr. Edinborough, never had any professional training as a teacher. In my opinion he is not qualified to criticize education in Ontario."

Ontario newspaper editors did not agree. The *St. Catharines Standard* took it up:

> *Last week in Sudbury at a convention a newspaper editor said that Ontario's teaching standards were declining.*
>
> *Last Saturday in the same place Education Minister Dunlop said there is neither an impending teacher shortage nor a lowering of teaching standards — not "one iota."*
>
> *He said that emergency summer courses for secondary school teachers were turning out highly qualified instructors, and that "supervisors and school principals say graduates of the summer courses are among their best teachers."*
>
> *Either Mr. Dunlop is right and a lot of teachers are wrong, or else Mr. Dunlop is talking the same hogwash that many cabinet ministers like to deliver. If his statement is true, and the summer course graduates are highly qualified and among the best teachers in the province, Mr. Dunlop could save a lot of tax money by doing away with the regular qualifying courses.*
>
> *Then Mr. Dunlop falls into the error which besets so many experts in their ivory towers. Referring to the editor who had the temerity to express the criticism, he says, "In my opinion Mr.*

Edinborough is not qualified to criticize education. He has never had any professional training as a teacher."

Yes, that's what the man said.

In effect, no man or woman may criticize anything to do with education unless he or she has had professional teacher training. (Short courses permitted, no doubt.) Home and School groups can fold up, and Education Week can be done away with, because if nobody can criticize, even constructively, why should anybody bother being interested? Why should newspapers give away all that free space for professional puffs telling us how good education is?

The converse of Mr. Dunlop's statement is that those who have had professional training as teachers have the qualifications to criticize the system. But either they aren't permitted to — or they don't dare.

The *Peterborough Examiner* was even more eloquent in its dismissal of Dunlop's point of view:

An interesting controversy has arisen between the Ontario Minister of Education, Mr. W. J. Dunlop, and the editor of the Kingston Whig-Standard, *Mr. Arnold Edinborough. In a speech at Sudbury Mr. Edinborough, an outspoken critic of Ontario education, said that the minister was embarrassed by declining standards in the teaching profession. Mr. Dunlop replied two days later that he was not embarrassed. On this subject Mr. Dunlop must, of course, rank as the world's foremost expert. If he says he is not embarrassed, he is quite clearly not embarrassed. Perhaps Mr. Edinborough meant that the minister ought to be embarrassed.*

But in refuting Mr. Edinborough's criticism, Mr. Dunlop ventured onto very swampy ground. He is quoted as saying: "In my opinion Mr. Edinborough is not qualified to criticize education. He has never had any professional training as a teacher." This is a stock reply that the Ministry of Education makes to its critics; if they are not graduates of the Ontario College of Education, they are quite likely to be called "laymen." A "layman" is a simpleton incapable of appreciating the mystique *of OCE.*

Before Mr. Edinborough became an editor he was a professor of English at Queen's University and at the Royal Military College. He was a very successful teacher. But he has no "certificate" from the Ontario diploma mill, and therefore in Mr. Dunlop's eyes he knows nothing about education. And that, we think, is one of the primary things that is wrong with education in this province: it is ingrown; it works on the principle of the engine which operates by consuming its own smoke. Its standards are not those of educated people the world over, but those which are determined by the OCE, which badly needs new blood and new ideas and a more exacting standard of scholarship. The OCE is the creature of the department, and the department is the creature of the OCE.

It is high time some fresh air was let into OCE, and frank criticism is one way of achieving this end. We may be sure that criticism will not come from OCE itself, and it is professionally disadvantageous for teachers to be too outspoken about it. Criticism, therefore, must come from outside the profession. Provincial education is everybody's business and, whatever Mr. Dunlop may believe, there are quite a few educated people in Ontario who take a keen interest in it, although they are not professionally engaged in teaching. Mr. Edinborough is prominent in this group, and what he has said about the decline of teaching standards is simply what many people — including many admirable professional teachers — know already.

Teachers themselves were glad to have a champion. They called the Department of Education in their bleaker moments the "mushroom factory," a place of total darkness whose product came mainly from horseshit.

I sympathized with them. They were under pressure from parents in the newly aggressive Home and School Associations. They were under pressure from trustees, nearly all of whom got elected by promising to keep taxes down. They were under pressure from students who, through television and other influences, were in training to be the hippies of the 1960s. They got no encouragement, enlightenment, or understanding from the department whose minister was totally out of phase with the times and in the hands of a theoretical bureaucracy whose members had not seen the inside of a classroom in years. And the teachers could do little about it. They were not a profession as they claimed to be — an issue I addressed in a radio talk on the CBC's country-wide network in March 1956.

I had put forward the marks of a professional: a thorough grasp of the theory and practice of his or her chosen field; a constant endeavour to improve that basic knowledge by the reading of the current literature; a high rate of pay to compensate for the hours spent in these nonfee activities; a tradition of service to the community at all times; and the right to set all these standards for any people aspiring to enter the profession.

This last was the stumbling block, even more than the others.

"The standards of education in Canada are fixed by politicians, not by teachers," I said over the CBC. "And since these standards are dictated from the provincial capital, it is natural that these standards for teachers are thus dictated, too. Just so long as the standards for teachers are set by a government department, there will never be a teaching profession in Canada."

The talk was reprinted in the *CBC Times*. It produced a raft of letters from across the country. But, alas, though improvements came in other areas of education, the teaching profession slid into becoming a teachers' union, a movement that spread from public education to colleges and universities. When I was writing and speaking so energetically — and over a period of fifteen years — I could see this coming. But the public did not until not only schools but community colleges and universities were, in the 1980s, all victims of teacher strikes.

Even the replacement of Dr. Dunlop very soon after all this, first by John Robarts, who became premier of Ontario, and then William Davis, who also became premier, could not stop this inevitable result.

XI

"AN AIR OF DEFEAT"

J UST AFTER I HAD MOVED TO THE *Whig-Standard*, Robertson Davies took off for a long summer vacation abroad. He asked me if I would take over the book reviews in *Saturday Night*, of which he was then literary editor, in addition to his full-time work at the *Peterborough Examiner*. I jumped at the chance.

Saturday Night was then in decline. For half a century it had been a major forum of ideas. Founded by Edmund Sheppard in 1884, it aimed specifically at the upper middle class for its readers. Sheppard's objective, he said in his introductory editorial, would be "to make the editorial columns of *Saturday Night* the most piquant and entertaining of any Canadian paper."

He had succeeded. Fred Paul, Hector Charlesworth, and B. K. Sandwell had carried on the tradition brilliantly. But by 1952 Consolidated Press, which owned *Saturday Night*, as well as a whole stable of special publications — *Canadian Grocer*, *Canadian Jeweller*, and such — was insolvent. Mrs. Sutton, the proprietor, sold the lot to Jack Kent Cooke, the brash owner of CKEY and the Toronto Maple Leaf baseball team.

Cooke bought it for *Saturday Night*, which he no doubt thought would bring him the prestige his radio riches had not. Still, under his ownership, Consolidated Press continued to lose money. But

Saturday Night was still a good place to publish and the pages normally filled by Robertson Davies were the best place in the magazine to be published. It also gave me a chance to review Rob's second novel, *Leaven of Malice*, a novel about a Kingston newspaper editor.

The arrangement worked well and, in 1958, Rob again asked me to do the summer reviews. By this time *Saturday Night* was publishing every two weeks instead of weekly and had dropped from its tabloid newspaper size to the size of *Maclean's* and *Time*, its competitors.

I liked *Saturday Night*. So did a lot of other people. We all wanted to see it thrive. I thought it might be a good idea to get the magazine involved in the education debate. It was a very hot topic, and they had no one writing about it. Instead, therefore, of sending my review of Richard Hoggart's book *The Uses of Literacy*, I took it into *Saturday Night's* offices, since I was in Toronto on *Whig-Standard* business, anyway.

As I always did when away from Kingston, I kept a diary:

July 22, 1957

In the afternoon to Saturday Night. *A rather worn-out makeshift bunch of offices and an air of defeat about the place. Marjoribanks, the new editor, is taken over from* Canadian Home Journal, *another in the Kent Cooke stud. How he and McManus, the managing editor, can ever make a go of it, I don't know.*

They asked me what I thought it should try to do. Suggested (1) articles on education (maybe might do some for them) (2) articles on the Commonwealth (3) wider variety of features.

In general, I said, an appeal to the literate and educated, whether they be teachers, doctors, or businessmen.

At no time then did I think of being more than a contributor to *Saturday Night*. I was too busy. Indeed, it was to meet with the provincial cabinet for a private briefing that I had come to Toronto. Afterwards I met with Bob Weaver, who was by now a good friend as well as a buyer of my scripts.

I had done a lot of work for *Wednesday Night*, the CBC's one night a week of literature, music, and art. I had also written several half-hour scripts for a series called *Letters and Papers*. These were dramatized personality profiles of writers. I had done one on John Keats and was now planning one on Arnold Bennett whose diaries fascinated me. I was impressed by his success, but a diary entry (I kept the Toronto diary going during the succeeding two weeks holiday on Garden Island) shows his output did not faze me:

> *I have been reading Arnold Bennett's journal, which is an excellent picture of a man who writes for a living. But the figure of words written, i.e., 250,000 or thereabouts per year, is not all that impressive to a journalist.*
>
> *I write about 1,000 words per day, 6 days a week = 6,000 x 50 a year = 300,000 words of editorial + 40 reviews of some 1,200 = 48,000 words. (All this for the* Whig.*) Plus speeches and special articles of maybe 10,000 per year. Total for one year: 358,000.*

No wonder my two-week holiday was being spent, the diary goes on to say, in "a pleasant mixture of swimming, eating, sleeping, and playing with the children." But there was also time for thought — and planning.

Toronto was the CBC's headquarters. It was the centre of publishing in Canada, and it was where I was constantly going to for television programmes and interviews with provincial ministers, editors, and such. In short, Toronto was nagging at me.

Diary for August 4:

Last Friday was my thirty-fifth birthday — halfway along, according to both the Bible and the latest insurance tables.

And where am I? Married, happily; three children, all intelligent so far and quite attractive [they were nine, seven and almost one at this point]. We have a house and a car, though the latter is more so in form than in function. Debts are large — on the house, on the year back in England in 1952-53, and because of the penury I existed in at the university. But income is growing and all may yet be well.

The Whig-Standard *is a good paper to edit, but it would be nice to be one's own boss.*

The income was growing because I was busy writing for the CBC, speaking to all sorts of groups and performing on CBC television, particularly on *Fighting Words*, the show hosted by Nathan Cohen on Sunday night. I was on it about every two months or so with such people as J. B. Priestley, Mort Sahl, Morley Callaghan (another quite regular member of the panel), Irving Layton, and Dr. Blatz, the controversial child psychologist.

A few months later I was asked by Bob Marjoribanks if I would become education editor of *Saturday Night*. I agreed and wrote three articles to appear in successive issues: curriculum, teacher training, and the Home and School movement.

In the fall of 1958 I was also working on a television script: *Generals in Politics*, the generals being Eisenhower and de Gaulle. I had conceived of it as a documentary, but Bob Weaver and Eric Koch, the two producers involved, had turned it into a docudrama with me as an editor on-screen. About two weeks before I was to go to Toronto to rehearse and do the show, I was rung by Gordon

Rumgay, the general manager of what was left of Jack Kent Cooke's publishing venture.

"I understand," he said on the telephone, "that you would like to be editor of *Saturday Night*."

"No. I understand from your call that you or Jack Kent Cooke would like me to be the editor of *Saturday Night*," I replied.

He waffled, but asked if I could come to talk with him about it. I said that I was due in Toronto in two weeks to do a show at the CBC and could see him then in between morning and afternoon rehearsals.

The *Generals in Politics* show was to be telecast on October 9. There was no tape in those days. We would rehearse in the morning and again in the afternoon. There would be a technical rehearsal late in the day, with airtime at 8:00 p.m. No tape. No editing. What you did was what the viewer got.

I had been a panelist on TV many times, but never an actor. For me it was a tense and draining morning.

Free at twelve noon (CBC unions at least kept producers to a schedule), I went from Studio IV on Yonge Street down to Cooke's offices at *Saturday Night* on Richmond Street. Rumgay wanted to talk about the offer, but I said I would prefer to speak directly with Cooke. I had never met him, but Grant Macdonald knew him and had told me that he was aggressive, sharp, and ruthless. Apparently, though, if you stood up to him, he was reasonable. I had no difficulty in meeting him on his level. He had initiated the inquiry. He wanted me. I, though flattered and keen, had a good job and did not need him.

We walked into his enormous, barnlike office, dominated by a model of *Pompadour*, the yacht that had brought him success at the Royal Canadian Yacht Club, but not acceptance.

"Arnold baby, how are you?"

"Fine, Jack. How are you?"

The interview was short.

"If I were to offer you the editorship of *Saturday Night*, would you take it?" he asked.

"On three conditions," I replied. "That you double my income, averaged over the past three years. That all other members of staff are on notice unless I reconfirm their position within three months. And that you do not read the magazine until it is on the newsstands."

"Okay," he said. "When can you start?"

"Two weeks Monday, provided you will pay the expense of an air taxi to get me here two days a week until December 31. I will move to Toronto on January 1, 1959."

"Done," he said. "Gord, work it out."

That was it. I had rehearsed the offer to myself several times between Rumgay's original call and this day. I had felt likely to take it if he met the conditions. Letty was, as she always was, supportive in what I thought would be best. I called her from a telephone booth on Yonge Street, and then went back to the CBC, rehearsed, did the show (the actor doing de Gaulle dried up and I had to feed him his lines), and left on the midnight train.

The journey was full of second thoughts: of Garden Island, our summer paradise, a mere fifteen minutes by ferry from the *Whig-Standard* office; of Little Picket, the English cottage-style house that Letty loved; of all our friends in Kingston who had welcomed us so well and made our Canadian immersion so much easier than it might have been; of the *Whig-Standard*, which I really liked and the Davies family, Senator Rupert, Arthur, and Rob, who had made my exit from academe so pleasant and worthwhile. I thought of all the offices I would have to relinquish: vice president of the Kingston Chamber of Commerce, director of the John Howard Society, and chairman of the New Symphony Association. But the die was cast.

The next day I met with Arthur Davies to tell him. "Well," he said, "we never expected to keep you forever. But we always thought you could do a job for us on the way up to something bigger."

I could have wept at such generosity of spirit. I told him about the deal.

"Take it," he said. "You'll make more there than I do here as publisher. You could never make that here."

We agreed on December 31 as my resignation date. The appointment was announced. People dropped into the office to congratulate me. The Reverend Dr. Shaw, professor at Queen's Theological College, author of twenty books, with flowing white mane and pince-nez on a ribbon, came in with words that I have remembered ever since. "Going to Toronto? *Saturday Night*? Congratulations. A word of advice from an old man. Do you be good, let he who will, be clever."

XII

THE BIG LEAGUES

F OR THE NEXT TWO MONTHS I flew to Toronto every Monday
and Friday, weather permitting, or went by the 3:00 a.m.
train if not.

The air taxi was an adventure. A Cessna 172, it flew from
Kingston airport when I got there, landed at Toronto Island
airport, and waited for me to get back to it in the late afternoon.
The flight took about two hours, though one day a strong head-
wind so slowed us down that the cars and trucks on Highway 401
below us gained on us. That evening we were back in Kingston in
just over an hour, thereby nearly landing on old Bill, who was
setting out the flares on the runway for us. The whole day cost
fifty dollars.

Noisy but convenient, the Cessna left my head ringing for the
first hour I was in *Saturday Night*'s offices. But it meant I could
edit both the *Whig-Standard* and *Saturday Night* for those two
hectic months.

I did not attempt to change much in those two months. I felt I
was merely there to write editorials, oversee the general article
mix, and choose the letters to the editor. Any major changes would
have to wait until I was there full-time. One thing I did was to
write a major article on the Crowe case. Harry Crowe, a professor
at United College, Winnipeg, had been fired from his position

because of remarks made in a private letter to a friend. By some chance the letter arrived on the principal's desk, and it was sent on to the proper addressee only after it had been opened, its contents read and, a note attached to it said, photocopied. The case became a cause célèbre in Winnipeg and, because United College was affiliated with the United Church, in Canada as a whole. The Canadian Association of University Teachers set up a committee to investigate, which proved that the General Council of the United Church had not investigated the matter at all, but had merely whitewashed the board and the principal, Wilfred Lockhart.

The affair had been the cause of a lot of rage and vehemence on Garden Island, where Professor Kenneth McNaught was a summer resident. Before he returned to *his* post at United College he had briefed me on the whole thing so that I could write about it in the *Whig-Standard*. It was a perfect, contentious, human rights, board versus faculty issue about which I had much privileged information.

The article got an immediate response. Letters poured in, not all of which were publishable. Phone calls came from United Church ministers. A number of people cancelled their subscriptions. It was all heady stuff for a new editor, and it carried me through an exacting time by pumping the adrenaline.

As soon as Christmas was over, I moved to Toronto. We had decided not to move the family until I had settled in a bit and had found a house we liked with schools to suit.

On January 4, Sunday, I took the six o'clock train to "Belleville, Port Hope, Oshawa, Toronto, and points west" to face the future. I had on a new black homburg hat that would, I thought, age me a little as well as keep my head warm in what was already a very cold winter. I had a week's change of clothing, a few books, and reservations arranged at the Albany Club. Then, like other gentlemen's clubs, it had guest suites in which members might stay for as long as a month.

As the train drew into Union Station at 9:30 on a cold winter's Sunday night, I looked out at sprawling big-city Toronto and had a fit of butterflies. I had read a lot about Canada. I had travelled the length and breadth of it. I had met a lot of people. I even knew some people in power, like Dana Porter, Billy Nickle, and a couple of others in the Ontario cabinet. As well, I had met the federal minister of justice, Stuart Garson, through Senator Davies.

For a thirty-seven-year-old immigrant only twelve years in the country, it was a start. But it seemed scarcely a powerful hand with which to start playing in the big leagues. *Saturday Night* was the big league. So, in his own way, was Jack Kent Cooke. I said to myself what an old man had said to me who was visiting my mother years ago, in another life, in another country. "Aim high. You can always hit low enough."

I started a diary the next day when I returned to the Albany Club after work:

> *First day at* Saturday Night. *The office was cold, the floor and furniture dirty, the whole project depressing. Mrs. Hutley had no desk, no typewriter, no supplies. The day ended in complete and unrelieved gloom.*

> *I missed L. and the family — I felt grubby and shabby and at odds with everyone.*

> *Living in the Albany Club is equally sterile. A poker game or bridge party in one room, perhaps a couple of billiards players upstairs, otherwise a tomb.*

Joan Hutley had been my secretary at the *Whig-Standard*, and by great good luck her husband, an army man, had been posted to Barrie effective January 1. She took a house there, commuted every weekend, and stayed in Toronto during the week. It was a heaven-sent gift. There would be at least one person I knew on the staff, and one I could trust. She also knew my habits and could save a lot of my time by winnowing correspondence and callers.

First I interviewed each staff member. That wasn't difficult, since there were only three. Herb McManus was well over fifty, conservative, set in his *Saturday Night* ways, unambitious, and methodical. He was pseudo-military to the core: he talked of MOs instead of doctors, padres instead of ministers, and made a fetish out of fussy self-discipline. He had the same sandwich-and-beer lunch every day at the same time at the same restaurant.

The business editor, Dick Baiden, was relatively unsophisticated but bright, aggressive, full of good ideas, and opposed to almost everything McManus stood for. McManus had difficulty handling him. He had even more difficulty handling the art director, a youngish, raffish man named Al Mercer. Bohemian in his ways, he came in late and hung over most of the time, but did not drink on the job and was keen to do new things with a new man. Irregular hours, unconventional habits, and a swift hand at layout made him anathema to plodding McManus.

They all welcomed me. We had a get-together lunch at the Savarin, then almost the only and certainly the best salad bar-buffet in town, just around the corner from our offices on Richmond Street West. Having talked to them, I went off to Ottawa to meet with Ed Copps, a brilliant ex-*Time* magazine writer who was now, at Jack Kent Cooke's invitation, our Ottawa editor, and two people who wrote regularly for us but not on staff — Robert Reford and Bob Mahaffy.

In Montreal Don Shepherd, the advertising manager, and I entertained some regular *Saturday Night* advertisers and their agency people. All very welcoming, all full of hope that *Saturday Night* would now be a livelier read than it had been. I sensed they would not increase their advertising, in fact, until it was.

Roy Tait was our Montreal man. We clicked straight away, and he was to prove a loyal, productive member of the organization all through my involvement with the magazine.

Staying at the Chateau Laurier in Ottawa where, my diary notes, I was greeted by name because I had been on the major Sunday television public affairs show the night before, and at the Queen Elizabeth in Montreal in a suite where we could entertain the advertisers, made the outlook a little less shabby than the offices in Toronto.

The real problem was that *Saturday Night* and *Liberty* were the only two publishing properties left to Cooke, and the offices of all the trade magazines he had sold to Maclean Hunter were empty — desolate, echoing spaces through which we approached our offices in the corner of the second floor.

Joan Hutley, as determined to make a success of the move as I was, had, in my absence, worked miracles. She had made the office gleam, changing furniture and making it look like home, which made me feel more confident that, as Cleopatra said in Shakespeare's *Antony and Cleopatra*, "all may be well enough."

Jack Cooke was a hard bargainer about helping me to buy a house in Toronto and made me sign a chattel mortgage for his cosigning of a note for the down payment. He also thought my plans for *Saturday Night*, as I had evolved them in the first two weeks, "ambitious."

God knows they were not revolutionary. All I was concerned about at the moment was that the editorials should come up-front instead of being buried at the back, and that we should give more space to letters. We would have to find a new book editor (or a stable of reviewers), since Robertson Davies had agreed, before my coming into the picture, to leave *Saturday Night* for the *Toronto Star*. The layout had to be better and the pictures crisper. We were still a fortnightly and we had to find good background writers to comment on issues rather than news. News was denied us. We wrote two weeks before publication, and the magazine stayed on the stands for two weeks after publication. We were always, therefore, a month behind the news.

We also had holdovers from the days when *Saturday Night* had been the Canadian business paper, a paper looked to for business analysis and advice before *The Financial Post* became so dominant. We had a question-and-answer column on insurance, and we had a similar and revered one on investment called "Gold & Dross." This still had some style to it:

Any market for Groundhog Gold Mines Limited?
—*T.H. Ottawa.*

Not a shadow of a bid for some time.

Any line on Gold Star Mines?
—*S.W. Brantford.*

Ceased twinkling many years ago.

What do you think of Orchan's chance at Mattagani?
—*C.F. Hamilton*

Only the rock knows the story.

The column also, in the first six months of 1959, advised its readers to buy uranium stocks for the long term, and to give solid thought to buying shares in Sherritt Gordon, Ford of Canada, Imperial Tobacco, Noranda, and Bell Telephone. The advice was tentative but based on neat, lucid profiles.

Our business editor, Dick Baiden, had a nose for news and kept the financial side lively in its feature articles. But the editorial mix was something of a dog's breakfast.

The January 31 issue, the first one in which I had brought the editorials up-front again under the title "Comment of the Day," had an article "New York Letter" by Anthony West, our New York correspondent, who was engaged in a lively argument with Senator Robert Kennedy about Jimmy Hoffa. There was also an article on Castro by John Harbron, one on merit pay for teachers, and a long piece by Dick Baiden on the bond market. Robertson Davies supplied a book review, sandwiched between an article on government financing of the export trade and the insurance column (about loan protection and hospital plans) and "Gold & Dross." Finally Mary Lowrey Ross reviewed daytime television and there was a travel piece on Barbados.

It seemed that we needed to cast our net deeper and not so wide; that we should give up financial Q&A columns; that we should have more political and national issue pieces.

Certainly we needed to change the layout. It was undistinguished in typography, heading, and pictures. Furthermore, the magazine's articles were bunched one after another up-front. Then, after the two-page opener, the reader was referred to a mass of continued on page so-and-so type filling the last few pages solid. And the advertising, it was pointed out to me both by Don Shepherd, the advertising manager, and by McManus, was a similar mix.

In that same January 31 issue the only four-colour ads were for liquor and cigarettes, and business ads — full-page corporate ads to small dividend notices — outnumbered the consumer side by something like three pages to one. Even in the spring book issue supplement, where four pages of book advertising kept seven pages of reviews apart, the overall count was business thirteen pages, consumer and cultural eleven.

This was all new to me. It was not like editing the *Whig-Standard*. Even the writing was different. What was written on Monday in Kingston was read by Tuesday noon and the phone often started to ring. At *Saturday Night* what was written this Monday was published two weeks hence. It was like publishing on the far side of the moon. Letters came in three weeks after the piece they commented on had been written.

However, there was an investigative piece on the waste in constructing the DEW line, material for which had been leaked to me after a casual conversation in the men's room of the Royal York Hotel in Toronto. This prompted the government to make noises about prosecution under the Official Secrets Act. There was also a savage piece about the Tory government's reluctance to act on the O'Leary Commission report.

The O'Leary Commission had been set up by the Liberal government to see what, if anything, could be done to protect Canadian publications from the influx of American magazines. Not only did American wholesalers dominate the newsstands (I was always rescuing *Saturday Night* from the back shelves and putting it prominently on display), but *Time* magazine printed a Canadian edition with editorial material already paid for in the United States. If a manufacturing company did this, it was called "dumping." The purpose of the O'Leary Commission was to highlight this practice and show how advertising was thus siphoned off into what was an essentially foreign product masquerading as Canadian.

I appeared, on behalf of Consolidated Press (*Saturday Night* and *Liberty*), before the commission in Ottawa, opening by saying, "The identity of Canada, its very existence as a nation, is what this Royal Commission on Publications is concerned with." I pointed out the penetration of the bookstalls that went unchecked while radio and television were protected by Canadian content quotas, and the restrictive practices indulged in by the American distribution agencies in controlling those bookstalls. I highlighted the dumping aspect of bringing in already written and paid-for magazines as mere vehicles for advertising revenue, most of which was therefore net.

I ended with a flourish: "The loss will not only be severe, it will be total. For if *Saturday Night, Liberty, Maclean's, Canadian Homes,* and *Chatelaine* — the last five national magazines now left — disappear, there will be no forum for Canadian national opinion. For Canadian letters to the editor do not appear in the Canadian edition of *Time*; Canadian articles rarely appear in the Canadian *Reader's Digest*; and the number of Canadian writers who are supported by both could be counted on the fingers of one hand. Yet it is they who are taking the advertising revenue that alone can support Canadian magazines. Without that revenue, decently and fairly competed for, Canadian magazines will die. And so, gentlemen, will Canada."

In constructing the brief for Cooke I had had access to his figures. In 1952 *Saturday Night* had lost $185,000. From 1953-1959 the loss on Consolidated Press's publishing operations was $1,660,742. These were large sums of money, even for Jack Kent Cooke. My five-bedroom house in South Rosedale had, in 1959, cost only $29,100.

It became clear to me that Cooke wanted out if he could get out. Rumours flew every week about the impending sale of *Saturday Night*. I had a hard enough time making it worthwhile reading. I did not need the constant nagging doubt as to whether it would still be published.

Cooke laughed at all the rumours. He kept his word, though, about reading it only after it had been published every fortnight. Occasionally he would phone me with a bouquet or brickbat. Once or twice he took me to lunch at the National Club where, as I tucked in, he would upbraid me as he ate a plate of clear soup, melba toast, and coffee.

A year after my move to Toronto he offered me a two-year contract with a salary increase of almost twenty percent over the period. In doing so he said that *Saturday Night* was now "getting somewhere in its long haul towards solvency" and that he felt I had had "a considerable hand" in its recovery.

Certainly the November 1959 issue, one year later than the one announcing me as editor, had more advertising pages and more colour pages than the 1958 one. The magazine was easier to read, thanks to a crisper layout. There were no turn pages. All articles started and ended in one place. There were new writers: Kenneth McNaught, John Gellner, Graham George (still head of music at Queen's), Jim Coleman, Donald Gordon, Jr., and Marcus Long.

We had had theme issues on the "Seaway, One Year After"; on postwar Canada, 1939-1959, with a commemorative look at the war itself; and on education, coinciding with the opening of school. The editorials were more numerous in September, and so were the letters they generated.

But it was a hard struggle. Cooke was not interested in the magazine. I had a travel budget for the year of only $2,500, and a promotion budget of $100 per issue. No one was paid more than $100 for an article. All our pictures were from agencies' stock or public relations firms. I longed to own the magazine myself. I was passionate about its potential. If I could get Cooke off the masthead and put some money together so that *Saturday Night* would have a fresh start, I felt life would be not just tolerable but exciting.

I tramped Bay Street, seeking such money. Canadian businessmen were not interested. Roy Thomson, whom I had got to know quite well in Kingston through his attending meetings of the television station in which he was a partner with Senator Davies, was quite blunt.

"When we take a position in something, Arnold, we take a majority position. If we had the majority position in *Saturday Night*, you would not like it, because we would want to run it our way. I doubt if that would be yours."

Then one morning a shortish man with balding head and thick, black-rimmed spectacles was shown into my office. His name was

Percy Bishop. I knew nothing about him. The only Percy Bishop I knew was a very different man — the head of Consumers Gas Company.

This Bishop came straight to the point. He would like to help me to buy *Saturday Night*. He had money and could call on more. He admired what I had done and would give me a free hand in developing a newly invigorated magazine. Would I be interested?

Of course I would. He seemed sincere: "*Saturday Night* is about the only thing we haven't sold out to the States," he said. "You work out a deal that makes sense and we'll do it."

When he left, I phoned a few people. None of them knew Percy Bishop. Paul Deacon, editor of *The Financial Post*, did. "He's a bucket shop operator. Flogs speculative mining stocks. He's under investigation in New Brunswick."

Another friend said that he had had difficulties with various security commissions, "but he is now in real estate in Mississauga. A shopping mall, I think."

It wasn't encouraging. But I persuaded myself that Jack Cooke had bought *Saturday Night* to see if its image would reflect on him in 1952. Maybe Percy Bishop was doing the same.

In mid-August — a hot August I remember — with the family away in Garden Island, I set to work on figures. Jack Cooke was forthcoming. I had spiked a deal he had had in the works with a very dubious figure named David Rush. Calling Rush just after his brother's bedroom was bombed by a rival businessman, I had told him that though the magazine was for sale, I was not. If he bought it, I would quit. I had then phoned Cooke and told him so, too.

So now it seemed we might do a deal. I had found the man, or at least he had found me. But Cooke was adamant about one thing: he would not sell *Saturday Night* without *Liberty*.

Liberty was a low-brow magazine — profiles of film and television stars, pop psychology, gossip, titillating advice, and so on. It was sold door-to-door by youngsters who vied for bonuses and prizes. The annual profit over the previous ten years had been about $53,000. Menacingly, though, its profit had slid $10,000 a year for the previous two years. Its circulation was in excess of half a million — an enormous liability.

Saturday Night, I discovered, now that I had access to the figures, had lost $1,191,000 in the previous nine years. I was pleased to note that since I had taken over as editor, the loss had been reduced from $134,000 in 1958 to $75,000 in 1961. There was then, in Consolidated Press, no net worth. What Bishop would be buying would be a marginally profitable magazine with a large annual budget, and a losing magazine with a much smaller budget. If we could reverse the trend in *Liberty* and accelerate the trend in *Saturday Night*, the deal might make sense.

After a lot of hard bargaining about projections of revenue and expense, and a totally surrealistic attention to inventory, which was nothing more than a lot of broken-down, shabby furniture, and a little more up-to-date accounting, printing, and typing machines, I suggested $250,000 as the purchase price. Bishop agreed, and a formal offer was made, with a closing date of August 31, over my signature, the payments to be spread over one year, the bulk of it in the first ninety days.

Cooke agreed. We set up a new company to take over the assets and names. In a fit of nostalgia I named it Fengate Publishing Limited, Fengate being the road that passed by the Lincolnshire farm where I had grown up in England. My mother was very pleased.

On September 1, 1959, *Time* magazine reported on the sale, ending its two-column story, with picture, thus:

> *As a publisher, Bishop evidently intends to rule with a light hand. In addition to editing* Saturday Night, *bearded, English-born Edinborough, thirty-nine, will become president of Fengate*

Publishing, which will be formed to take over the two magazines.
"Saturday Night should be changed," Bishop said. "It's losing
money, and I don't like losing money. Arnold will decide what
has to be done."

Edinborough, who came to Saturday Night *in 1958, will have*
authority over the low-brow Liberty, *as well, but plans no*
changes in its profitable formula (August's lead story: "How I
Became TV's Hawaiian Eye *Tootsie"). Beyond his hope to bolster*
Saturday Night's *thin staff, he gave no hint of his plans, except*
to exude confidence in the result. "This has been a holding
operation until now," he said. "It won't be anymore. We're going
to be a power in this country."

XIII

THE NEW
SATURDAY NIGHT

I T WAS ALL VERY HEADY AND EXCITING. Letters of congratula-
tion came from all over. Lester Pearson, then leader of the
Opposition, wrote. Frank McEachren, aide-de-camp to the
lieutenant governor, wrote. Arthur Hailey wrote and offered
his services. The chief parks naturalist of Canada wrote. So did
a score of others, notably four or five heads of advertising
agencies.

Cocky? Of course I was cocky. I wrote to Duncan McTavish,
the Ottawa lawyer who had chaired the Liberal Party convention
that had elected Pearson leader and been helpful in early talks with
Cooke:

*As time progressed, it seemed that Cookie-boy responded to the
deep-freeze treatment because we eventually had to pay much
less then he was asking. I am sure that you helped in bringing
him round . . . and I want to thank you for it.*

*Bishop is a mercurial and puckish character and a real maverick
in the money marts. He has had a fair amount of mud slung at
him, but I think his heart is in the right place — in fact, I am
sure it is.*

As the deal is set up, he provides money on a yearly basis and I run the whole thing. I also will be allowed to buy into the company almost as much as I want to and can afford to. In fact, I sometimes wonder if I'm not living in a perpetual Santa Claus environment.

Of Bishop's hidden agenda, I twigged nothing. Nor did I have to. He *did* provide money, he did let me run things, and I plunged right in. The writing and editing was, for the moment, second to administration. We had to find new offices, and did so at 55 York Street, right next to the Royal York Hotel. We took two floors, and when shown the plan for the disposition of offices, noted my own corner office, gave a look at the rest, and initialled it. Within an hour I had a memo on my desk from Arthur Phillips, the circulation director:

I am very dissatisfied with the distribution of space in the new quarters.

I agree that we would require about 15,000 square feet, but the mathematical wizard that decides it should be divided down the middle with workers and machinery squeezing into one-half the space and the executives taking the other half must not have been taught anything beyond the one-half fraction.

To place about 17 executives and 10 assistants in 7,500 square feet would allow each person a working space of 275 square feet. The best office manuals suggest 120 square feet per person with an allowance of 250 square feet per person for top management.

Forty workers with machinery and a stockroom naturally will require more than the 120 square feet allowed for an office worker.

Personally it does not make any difference to me, but workers are not quite as dumb as they were a few years back and resent being in crowded conditions when other employees of the same firm have ample area.

On the same desk was already a long memo from Frank Rasky, the editor of the successful (and profitable) *Liberty* magazine. Quite reasonably he suggested that he be given a raise in salary "more commensurate with the energy I put into my joyful task, and that in the face of an appallingly low budget and minuscule staff"; that he be confirmed as editor in chief with "paramount authority over the editorial department of *Liberty*"; and that he be permitted a "profit-sharing equity" in the magazine.

These were not decisions I had ever faced, but whatever those decisions were, they seemed to work.

We all fitted into the new offices, and Rasky continued to put out an effective and popular magazine with writers whom *Saturday Night* would have liked to have had. Gordon Sinclair, Hugh MacLennan, Hugh Garner, Tom Alderman, John Wilcox, all appeared in the first issue of *Liberty* under the new management. Joyce Davidson also wrote for the magazine, and Peter Whalley did illustrations. Frank Rasky did a series on the pioneers of the Canadian West (later collected into a book) and, with the joyful energy he had mentioned in his memo, had his picture taken interviewing Carol Channing, Liberace, Gypsy Rose Lee, Nat King Cole, Mike Nichols, and Elaine May — all in a period of six months.

No, *Liberty* was not a problem. Rasky knew exactly what he was doing. His staff cooperated with energy, and the advertising flowed in — twenty pages in October, thirty-three in November, twenty-three in December — most of it four-colour. So I turned my energies to what I thought I knew best — *Saturday Night*.

Editorially we had made great strides since I joined the

magazine. In the issue that announced the new ownership there were articles by Stuart Keate, then publisher of the *Victoria Times*; Desmond Morton of Osgoode Hall; Donald Gordon, CBC correspondent in London; Frank Drea, a *Toronto Telegram* writer who later became an Ontario cabinet minister; and three articles on education by people actively concerned with it. John Gellner and Professor Kenneth McNaught had been added to the roster of contributing editors, and Kildare Dobbs was writing regularly.

What *Saturday Night* lacked, I thought, was promotion. Cooke had allowed only $2,400 per year — $100 per issue. I had tried to buttress that by speaking, all across the country, on a variety of topics and on both radio and television. Bishop agreed to a promotion budget of $40,000, and we immediately hired Batten Burton Durstine and Osborn as our public relations consultants. Of their two major thrusts, one was very successful, the other chintzy.

The chintzy one involved a series of ads in selected newspapers with me in a variety of outlandish situations. I was photographed in heavily thoughtful pose between two people, one masked as Khrushchev, the other as John F. Kennedy; on a flying carpet with a tarboosh on my head; drawing a moustache on a picture of Prime Minister Diefenbaker; in a safari suit with topee; and wrapped in ticker tape.

All this was supposed to show *Saturday Night*, through me, as unconventional, irreverent, and daring, and for advertisers, involved in business, travel, politics, and the arts (I was also seen inspecting a pseudo Henry Moore). I felt a fool doing the photo shoots and looked one when the ads came out. The campaign probably turned off some readers, and almost certainly some advertisers.

The other idea was more productive. Together with BBDO, CTV, and CNCP Telecommunications we became sponsors of a new network show called *Telepoll*. The idea, developed by Ted Cott in New York, was simple. A pertinent issue of the day was backgrounded in the first segment of the show. Then selected respondents in cities across the country voted yea or nay for a resolution debated by a panel in the second segment, their votes being transmitted directly back to CFTO by CNCP technology. Lifting these results off the telex machine, I then had the last segment in which to announce the results of this public opinion sample and interpret them.

It was an upbeat show. It was based on what was then new technology. (Thought for the day: telex is only thirty years old, and the fax machine has already made it obsolete.) It dealt with issues of national importance, and *Saturday Night* was clearly right up-to-the-minute in dealing with them.

We asked whether Canadians thought the United Nations should intervene, by armed force of its members, in civil war. Over half said it should. We asked whether Britain's joining the European Common Market would weaken the Commonwealth. The majority of respondents said no. We asked whether Canada should send troops to India if China were to invade. A whopping fifty-three percent said yes, though forty-eight percent said even if we did, we should still sell wheat to China, then one of our biggest customers.

Our best and most controversial programmes were on domestic affairs. When we debated the question whether doctors should be allowed to give children blood transfusions even when their parents, through religious conviction, denied their assent, Glenn How, counsel for the Jehovah's Witness sect, walked off the set in a rage. The vote was crushing to him: eighty-three percent said doctors should. Widening the range of causes for divorce (Canada still at that time only permitted adultery or insanity as causes) was widely approved. So was off-track betting and the expenditure of tax money to help keep notable artists in the country (a propitious vote for the newly founded Canada Council).

What seems wistful now, in looking back, is the question of Quebec. In January 1962 the largest majority on any question we had ever asked was whether Quebec should become a separate state: eighty-six percent said no and seventy-nine percent said such an event was totally unlikely.

There was one intriguing afternoon at CFTO when we invited Marshall McLuhan to participate. The great guru of communications had not up to then been involved in television, except when interviewed on a talk show. He was stunned when he saw the running script we gave him. That all this half hour was actually programmed to the last second was a total revelation to him. And he was appalled when he heard the cost of a thirty-second ad — and how it had to fit exactly.

The show got a lot of press. The ratings were good, and Royce Frith, now Senator Royce Frith, was the perfect, pipe-smoking host. (Another thought for the day: pipe smoking was a mark of sober, considered reflection.) For eighteen weeks, all through the winter and spring of 1961-62, I barrelled up the partly completed Don Valley Parkway every Saturday afternoon to CFTO, listening to the opera quiz, did the show, and came back to the sports results on radio in the car.

CFTO was new. *Telepoll* was new. *Saturday Night* was old, but in a new phase.

We had also redesigned *Saturday Night*. The front cover was now divided perpendicularly down the middle. A strong photograph illustrative of a leading article took the right-hand half; a list of the main articles in a new and arresting typeface took the left.

We got the startling photos cheap through the ingenuity of Al Mercer, the art director. The first such, on the December 9 issue, was a close-up of Pablo Picasso taken, quite legitimately, from the book *Picasso's Picassos*, which led off the Christmas book section. The second, on the December 23 issue, was a hilarious illustration of Tiny Tim on Scrooge's shoulders by Ronald Searle — again taken from a new edition of *A Christmas Carol*, characterized by the reviewer as "the thousand and first new edition" of Dickens's work.

Certainly by mid-February, six months into the new regime, things at Fengate looked good. Kildare Dobbs had joined us as an associate editor and had brought his own wry and spritely vision to articles, book reviews, and the new design. It was he who brought in Carl Dair to do it. (Said Dair when we met: "I'm glad to meet you. The person I've been dealing with, Kildare, has a name I find menacing.")

Dick Baiden, now promoted to associate editor, was doing a lot more of the editorial spadework, writing editorials for "Comment of the Day," seeking out contributors, but still keeping his finger on the public pulse.

The Christmas edition of 1961 had pieces by Hugh Mac-Lennan, Robertson Davies, Ethel Wilson, Diana Goldsborough, William Allister (a remarkable diary from a Canadian in a Japanese prison after the fall of Hong Kong), Kildare Dobbs, and the still peerless Mary Lowrey Ross.

The joy of the season was somewhat marred by an ugly scene on Nathan Cohen's show *Fighting Words*. I had been a constant guest on the show for five years, so did not think anything about it when invited to participate on the Sunday before Christmas. I had my first twinge of doubt, though, when Tony Emery, a critic from Victoria, appeared in the makeup room. He had written a scathing review of Morley Callaghan's new novel *A Passion in Rome* for our Christmas book section. "I have always found Morley Callaghan an outstandingly dull writer, even in a national litera-ture that seemed to be overcompensating guiltily for having produced a Leacock," he said at the beginning of his review. He had gone on from there. Callaghan had a "tin ear" for speech; a "total lack of any sense of dialogue"; and his style was characterized as that "glossy-magazine, 'hearts and flowers played in thick woollen gloves on a wheezy harmonium' prose."

My sense of chill increased when no one else joined us. Obviously the two other participants were being kept away from us. When we walked onto the set (and remarkably this was live, not tape), there were Morley Callaghan and Ralph Allen. The first quote we responded to was harmless, then came one about critics, and the fur began to fly. There was a prominent vein in Morley's forehead that bulged and throbbed. He poured venom on Emery, who fought back. Ralph Allen announced that this being a private war he would stay out of it. I, when challenged by Callaghan as printing the review to sell copies, replied that I thought a review of a Callaghan book was not a grabber for the average reading public, not even *Saturday Night*'s public.

It was great public television and privately, a shocking, emotional upset. At the end of the show Callaghan stamped out, and though, together with Mary Lowrey Ross, we had shared many a Saturday night at his house up to now, he did not speak to me for four years afterwards. His son Michael, an account executive with MacLaren Advertising, rang me up and offered to punch me out.

Life was full and exciting. Letty, whose name had so often been misunderstood as Betty, changed to Tish, and has been so known in Toronto ever since. She was involved with Planned Parenthood as volunteer PR person, but would also go off, as her by now-adolescent son put it, almost anywhere with a bucket of spermicidal foam on her arm to a birth control clinic. Since the advising of birth control, and the publicizing of its devices, was illegal, Sarah, at six years old, invented a marching song the family would sing as we picketed the prison where any day, Sarah thought, her mother might be incarcerated.

Kippy, the other daughter, was now at the National Ballet School, where she had been accepted, although her short tendons made pliés agony and the likelihood of a ballet career remote.

"But, Daddy," she said when hearing the news, "wouldn't it be wonderful if I turned out to be the first ballerina *ever* with short tendons."

In fact, she was admitted, as some others were, because her fees were important to the budget and her character would make a lively difference to the small academic classes. And though she never did become a ballerina, she did have a good acting career and has for years now earned her very adequate living as the owner of a ballet-theatre school in London, Ontario. The discipline and professionalism of the National Ballet School were formative and lasting elements in her later life.

But there were clouds on the horizon. *Saturday Night* was blooming editorially, but the advertising was slow to increase while the promotion and travel budget soared. Bishop had said that he would leave me alone, but budgets spoke louder than good intentions. We had monthly meetings about the finances of Fengate, and a memo of April 4, 1967, shows that things were getting serious:

Dear PW:

I know that the position of both Liberty *and* Saturday Night *has given you some cause for concern in the past two or three weeks.*

It may not be much consolation, but the following figures show that at least Fengate is further ahead than anyone else in the magazine game. The following figures appeared in the lineage summary of the Magazine Advertisers' Bureau of Canada for the year to date.

Canadian Homes — *down 20 percent*
Chatelaine — *down 14 percent*
Maclean's — *down 16 percent*
Reader's Digest — *down 16 percent*
Time — *down 11 percent*
La Revue Populaire — *down 34 percent*
Saturday Night — *down only 9 percent*
Liberty — *down only 5 percent*

I know it isn't much to be top of the flunks, but it does show that we are selling harder and achieving more than even the big boys who have been in the business for a lot longer than we have.

Yours sincerely,
Arnold Edinborough
President

I was also aware, through an article in *The Financial Post* on October 27, 1961, that Bishop proposed to found another magazine called *The Canadian*. To be edited by Arthur Lowe, an elderly journalist, it was to be dedicated to free enterprise. It was to be financed through a stock issue of Continental Industrial Holdings, the holding company that also owned Fengate. Rumour had it that this stock was peddled at Social Credit meetings in Alberta, where the name of the Brown brothers, Robert and Frank, gave the transaction some authenticity. The assets of the company were two coal leases and the three publications, *Saturday Night*, *Liberty*, and *The Canadian*.

On May 11, 1962, after some trouble with the Alberta Securities Commission, Bishop reported to me that he had not raised the equity cash he had sought, that Fengate was losing too much money, and that he needed to straighten things out.

He then called in Harold Cook, his right-hand man and treasurer of Fengate, plus another man I had never seen. All, with my exception, waived right of notice for a shareholders' meeting at which Cook was declared president of Fengate and I was demoted to vice president.

Oh, well, I thought, maybe a financial man should run the whole company. I would be able to give more time to *Saturday Night*.

I had already been in Montreal, chasing advertising almost weekly. I had had two longish visits to New York, where I watched the advertising manager of Cunard White Star drink two double martinis, two glasses of wine, and a brandy at lunch, after which he returned dead sober to his office and said he would look at our presentation favourably.

So, with Cook's agreement, I now flew off to London to see the travel people there, the Distillers' Company, Schweppes, and a few advertising agencies that still controlled the promotion of British firms in Canada.

On June 11 I got a cable from Dick Baiden: "Learn confidentially Satnight Canadian to merge stop July 7 last issue Satnight stop Staff to be discharged expectable June 15 stop Urge return soonest. Baiden."

I was back in Toronto in twenty-four hours and found all to be true. I tried to put together a group that would buy *Saturday Night* but, of course, in seven days it was impossible. I told Bishop I wanted nothing to do with the *Canadian Saturday Night*, especially when he offered me a two-year leave of absence at full salary as long as I would keep my name on the masthead and not go into the office. I told him what I had told Jack Kent Cooke earlier: the magazine might be for sale, but I was most emphatically not.

So I quit. So did Baiden. So did Dobbs, and Gellner had already been fired in my absence. The papers and television were full of it. *Time* magazine quoted my final remarks: "*Saturday Night* as we knew it is dead. Kaput." To Bishop I said, "You will be bankrupt in a year."

Then I went to ground. Arthur Hailey immediately offered his cottage in the Kawarthas as a resting place — "until the dust settles," he added.

When it did, with a most welcome letter in my briefcase, we then went off to Garden Island to regroup.

XIV

A SECOND CHANCE

G ARDEN ISLAND WAS THE CENTRE of our summer lives from 1954 to 1987. A small island opposite the Kingston Yacht Club, it was owned by the Calvin family whose forebears had acquired it in the late 1830s. Originally they used it as a base from which to forward squared timber brought in schooners from the upper Great Lakes in huge rafts down the St. Lawrence to Quebec. When canals made such rafting obsolete, the family got into shipbuilding. But the yard was summarily closed at the outbreak of World War I.

Since then the Calvin family members used the island as a summer place only and had invited a few outside people to lease those houses for which they had no family tenants. The houses, most of them built in the last quarter of the nineteenth century, were ramshackle, commodious, and mysterious enough in size and shape to enthrall the younger members of the family. Apart from the houses, it was an ideal summer place and scarcely a mile from the Kingston shore.

There was a wood deep enough and far enough from the houses to get deliberately lost in. There was a meadow with wild straw-berries and raspberries. There was an old barn near a south-facing beach of smooth rock. There was an uninterrupted shoreline facing north where one could swim, dive, fish, go boating in the rowboat, or sail in the Albacore.

There was no telephone except in a little hut about fifty yards from our house, itself an extension of the telephone in the Calvin White House at the foot of the island. Goods were brought up from the ferry dock by wheelbarrow or handcart. A ferry called in four times a day, and Captain Lyle Dougan's water taxi was open twenty-four hours a day from spring breakup to fall freeze-up. It was, for us and our children, the one constant residence to which everyone came, long after they ceased to be children. In fact, all three brought their own children to the island as the years passed.

It was a soothing place that hot summer of 1962, which put *Saturday Night*, *Liberty*, Fengate, Percy Bishop, and company out of our minds. And instead of fishing, swimming, playing Scrabble, and reading for just a couple of weeks, that year I spent the whole summer on the island. Or most of it.

The letter that had arrived just the day before we left Toronto was from Norman Mackenzie, president of the University of British Columbia. Our friend, Geoff Davies, was one of his assistants, and I had met Mackenzie — Larry, his friends called him — on several occasions.

He started his letter straight to the point, a habit that even a lifetime in the academic world, almost half as president, had not changed.

Dear Arnold:

Would you be interested in spending a few years with the University of British Columbia?

Geoff Andrew [his executive assistant] and I have felt that our universities do not pay enough attention to the mass media and particularly to the press which, for better or worse, are probably

our most important educational institutions. We have persuaded
Don Cromie to assist us with an experimental programme over
a period of five years. He has agreed to provide up to $15,000 a
year for the first three years and at least $10,000 for the next
two. What we need is someone of your distinction and experience
who might lecture to students both for credit, in order to ensure
an audience, and for the fun of it, by way of providing informa-
tion. This could mean a course in the Department of English on
"The Press as Literature" or "The History of the Press" or
something of the kind. It could mean a more general series of
lectures to the students in education who will be going out as
teachers throughout the province. It could mean a series of
general lectures under the auspices of our Department of Uni-
versity Extension.

I was out of a job, and though I had become passionate about
making *Saturday Night* work and had loved journalism from the
moment I stepped into the *Kingston Whig-Standard* office, I still
missed the university.

At the *Whig-Standard* it had not been too bad. Queen's was
close, and I still had all kinds of contacts there. But at Toronto,
what with television, radio, and public speaking, as well as *Satur-*
day Night (and latterly *Liberty*), I had almost no contact with the
university except for Professor John Irving, who was on the
editorial board of *Saturday Night* when I arrived in 1959.

Moving to Vancouver was not unattractive. Its climate, its
gardens and, indeed, its general ambience, were much closer to
England than Ontario's. We were still young: I celebrated my
fortieth birthday on Garden Island that summer. The two younger children would not find new schools difficult — neither was
yet out of the elementary system. Kip, the National Ballet School
student, could go into residence if she so wished. I also thought
that a Press Research Institute could be established. There was no

valid, consistent research being done on the media. No historical perspective on the evolution of Canada's press had been done outside a few individual studies.

I agreed to fly out to Vancouver and meet with the committee of deans in mid-July, taking a fully worked-out scheme for a press research institute with me. Basically it would be set up under the UBC umbrella, would have the kind of courses Mackenzie had mentioned, but would also have a research facility — ad hoc for professional journalists, as well as postgraduate for the more academic enquiries. I undertook, if the scheme were approved, to raise money from the newspaper owners, publishers, and radio/television companies in Toronto, all of whom had interests on the West Coast.

The meetings went well, though the English department was leery of a stranger coming into their midst, especially at the agreed salary, which was that of a full professor, the money coming directly from the grant by Donald Cromie.

As Professor Roy Daniels warned me: "I have been assuming that your primary task here will be to establish the Press Institute, that you will be able to offer a course on the history of 'journalism' in its more literary contexts, and that we should give very careful thought to the Renaissance as a field in which you might wish to do something. This last is a very touchy internal problem for this department, but I am sure we can work it out."

The final agreement was that my appointment would run from September 1, 1962, to June 30, 1965. It was also agreed that I should spend the first part of the academic year, which had already started by the time I was appointed, in Toronto, fine-tuning the design of the institute and calling on people who might consider helping towards its funding. I would go out to Vancouver at the beginning of January. Again, as when we moved to Toronto, Tish would not come with me until I had found a house, and until the children had finished their respective school years.

The announcement of my appointment was widely covered in the media. A Canadian Press story was reprinted in almost every Canadian daily, since Don Cromie was news, and so was his initiative. Letters poured in again from those who had once praised the Fengate takeover at *Saturday Night*, then commiserated on its demise, and now wished me well in a new venture.

My membership on the board of the John Howard Society of Ontario was transferred, with my consent and at the B.C. Board's request, to the John Howard Society of British Columbia. Nathan Cohen, now entertainment editor of the *Toronto Star*, asked me to do a column each Saturday from Vancouver for his special section. Don Cromie asked me to do a column at the bottom of the *Vancouver Sun*'s editorial page each Monday. And Bob Weaver was keen to get more *Letters and Papers* scripts for CBC's *Wednesday Night*.

What had been a simple academic commitment for two years at Queen's had certainly mushroomed in the subsequent fifteen years. Canada *was* a land of opportunity. It welcomed newcomers, even critical newcomers, with enthusiasm. Maybe a little too much enthusiasm.

Our circle of friends and acquaintances had grown to include people in almost every city in Canada, even people whom we had never met but felt they knew us from *Saturday Night* or television.

Even so I had qualms about the welcoming climate at UBC. I was not an academic, although I had been one and had the necessary qualifications to pass credential muster. I was already on staff, but had not met more than a couple of people in the department of which I had been a member for four months when I arrived in January. I was being paid for by an outside source at a salary greater than my official rank of associate professor entitled me to.

I need have had no such doubts. The faculty at UBC were uniformly friendly. I had known Geoff Davies since 1947 when we taught together at Queen's Summer School. Ron Jeffels, another assistant to the president, had sought my advice before going from the University of Alberta to my old college in Cambridge in 1948. Earle Birney had been enthusiastic about the *Cataraqui Review*, and Bill Nicholls, professor of religious studies, had read my columns in the *Canadian Churchman* with approval. Ron Baker, an academic planner, had come out to UBC on the same boat in which we had crossed the Atlantic in August 1947.

Saturday Night had been complimentary about the Vancouver International Festival that Nicholas Goldschmidt had been running against all odds for three years now. The Playhouse Theatre, wishing to turn entirely professional, asked me almost on arrival to join their steering committee.

I found a small apartment just off the university campus but well inside the university lands. It was lonely without Tish and the family, but people conspired to keep me busy and happy.

Geoff Davies put his car at my disposal once a week for shopping, and on many other occasions he and Vera, his wife, made the domestic side of life very bearable. And when Vera and I went to buy a bed for my apartment, the confusion of the salesman when he found we were not buying one to share was so hilarious that it made a good *Vancouver Sun* column.

At the *Sun* Alexander Ross was the op-ed page editor with whom I dealt about my column, and Paul St. Pierre was the editorial page editor. They nicely balanced the academic side each week.

But it was the university where I mostly lived, taking most of my meals in the Faculty Club. The memory of morning coffee discussions with Bill Nicholls, Walter Hardcastle, Ron Jeffels, Dean Chant, and a host of others is still warm. The talk was informed, often witty, sometimes caustic, and always, in memory at least, about ideas not people. I had missed that at *Saturday Night*.

But the Press Research Institute was not going so well. Larry

Mackenzie had written me on June 29 and retired as of July 1. The acting president, Dean Chant, was very warm towards the idea. The new president, John Macdonald, when he arrived from his Harvard dentistry department, was not. Time and time again I sought an interview with him. Geoff Davies, now the principal assistant to the president, also did his best. But no appointment ever came about.

What Macdonald had done soon after he arrived had been to imply that Premier W.A.C. Bennett was not only uninterested in the university's financial plight in the face of greatly increased enrollment, but that his disinterest was "stupid." Bennett said nothing but held the university grant so far down that a moratorium was declared on all new courses. It did no good for me to point out (in writing since he would not see me) that the institute was to be privately financed, as my own appointment was at the moment.

This was very discouraging, even though the rest of my time was so pleasant. There were walks with Harry Adaskin down the long avenue to the university lands entrance, with tea at the teahouse just outside. I saw *Aida* with Bob Phillips, president of the Vancouver Opera, and John Prentice, later to be chairman of the Canada Council, who, walking out at intermission, allowed that he thought the roly-poly Mexican soprano singing Aida was "a trifle less than celestial." There were meetings with Joy Coghill, Michael Johnston, and Bob Phillips at Bob's house, planning the first professional season of the Playhouse Theatre. And there was night after night at the desk in the apartment, researching and writing the long-abandoned *Revels of Henry VIII.*

Rain. Oh, yes, rain. By the third week of January I feared I would grow webs between my toes. Then all through February came warm sun, crocuses, daffodils, irises even, while Tish wrote of her struggles with deep snow in the driveway.

I went back east for Easter, aptly enough, thereby enjoying a mild Ontario spring while the rain came down in sheets in Vancouver. By the end of April, when rain came to Toronto, it was tanning weather in British Columbia, followed by cloudless May, roses, blue sky, hot sun.

The cloud over the institute would not go away, though. So when I returned to Toronto on June 1 (when it rained so hard in Vancouver, they could not roast the ox for the opening of the International Festival), the future was a little uncertain.

Then Cy Laurin, vice president of Maclean Hunter, rang me up. "Arnold, are you really committed to going to Vancouver?"

"Why?"

"Since you say why and not yes, can I come and see you?"

Which he did.

Bishop, he said, was in dire straits. Although the current issue of the *Canadian Saturday Night* had an article in it saying he was poised to buy out the Murchison interests in the Trans-Canada Pipeline, he was strapped for cash. Murray Printing would not print another issue until they were paid.

Would I be interested in paying the printing bill, in getting *Saturday Night* back? Maclean Hunter was concerned about the implementation of the O'Leary Report. If *Saturday Night* and *Liberty* collapsed, any implementation would seem to be pandering to one firm.

"With what would I buy it?" I asked.

"With money guaranteed at the Toronto Dominion Bank," Laurin replied.

"And with what would I run it?"

"With advertising revenues. Maclean Hunter would print it and defer any payment for at least a year."

Tish and I talked it over. It seemed too good to be true in one way. But in another it was horrendous. Our house had been sold, with possession on July 1. Our cottage on Garden Island had been sublet for the whole summer. We had an agreement to rent a house on Vancouver's West Eighth Street. Our joint application was in for the Point Grey Golf Club. I had agreed to be host of the 7:00 p.m. after-the-news television show on CBC Vancouver, and I had become chairman of the Playhouse Theatre.

As the Maclean Hunter/*Saturday Night* negotiations gradually came to a head, these other things had to be addressed.

The owner in Vancouver did not mind. He had another tenant in the wings. Doug Collins took over the 7:00 p.m. television slot (and did it for years). We never have taken up golf.

Meanwhile, we went to farewell party after farewell party in Toronto, including a "house-cooling" party organized by Serell Hillman, the *Time* correspondent who knew something was afoot but could never pin it down (and never did discover who backed the deal).

Then, on June 29, the announcement was made. Percy Bishop, who had been dealing only with lawyers, asked at last to meet with the principals. I shall never forget the look on his face when I walked in and said, "You were looking for the principals, Percy? I'm them. Out."

The next day, as we were packing up the house, Adele Deacon, wife of the editor of *The Financial Post*, who lived just around the block from us, came to the door.

"There you are, my dears. The keys. We've gone for the summer except for Paul. Please use the house for as long as you need it."

It really did feel as though we were now home for good.

Maclean Hunter needed *Saturday Night* to continue. Despite all its ups and downs from 1952 onwards, it was still almost an icon in Canada. People who had never read it thought they had, and dozens of people would say to us that their parents had always read it. If *Saturday Night* could keep going, then legislation that would level the playing field between the *Time* and *Reader's Digest* American dumpers and the *Maclean's/Chatelaine* group would not look as though it were protecting the profits of one company.

Why did I need it? That was a very different question. It was not vindictiveness towards Bishop, although there was a certain ignoble sense of triumph in giving him and his cronies their marching orders. It was not to stay in Toronto. Vancouver had been very welcoming. University life had its unmistakable charm in 1963, when sit-ins and student radicalism were still far off. The climate of British Columbia and its scenery were both, compared to flat Ontario and its vicious winters, desirable.

No. There was a passion to make *Saturday Night* be what it had been before: an articulate, liberal, civilized commentator on Canadian affairs. In a sense, that was also a passion for Canada, which had taken us quickly, eagerly, into its mainstream. In sixteen years I had gone from a raw immigrant to a national figure, listened to by decision-makers in a country of which, when I landed in Halifax in August 1947, I knew nothing. On the way my salary had increased tenfold, from $2,400 a year as a lecturer at Queen's to $25,000 a year now as editor and publisher of *Saturday Night*.

My two oldest children were at the very best schools they could wish to be at. Kip was immersed at the National Ballet School, whose academic standards, like its ballet standards, were impeccable and maintained in both areas by a student-teacher ratio that was almost one-on-one. Alastair was at Upper Canada College where, despite its hoary elite image, he was comfortable playing on the league-leading football team and, at the same time, organizing a poetry and music festival. Sarah, the youngest, was at Whitney Public School, part of a group of friends that has survived past university.

For Tish things had been difficult. I was away from home a lot. Even at Queen's I had been filling invitations to speak, first in Ontario, then later all over the country. She had been alone with all three children for six months while I was in Vancouver — two of whom at thirteen and fifteen were not at their most docile years.

I had become part and parcel of Canada. For me it had certainly been a land of opportunity. For her, bringing up a family in an alien culture and foreign country, it had been more of a sentence than an opportunity. But the volunteer work with the symphony orchestra in Kingston, and with Planned Parenthood in Toronto, which called on her nursing training, had given her an outlet beyond the home and a part in helping to mould a changing society.

For Canada was changing. The Stratford Festival was, in 1963, ten years old and an undoubted success. (Its season was the front cover of the first *Saturday Night* after I returned.) The Vancouver International Festival, unfortunately so far ahead of its time that it collapsed under its financial burden, was a foretaste of things to come. Already a celebration of Canada's centenary was being planned, and its first expression was the Confederation Centre of the Arts in Charlottetown.

Politically, though Diefenbaker and Pearson squared off at each other all through the sixties, the Créditistes and Social Credit Party had shown that there were alternatives, even though those particular ones were not attractive to too many people. And in Saskatchewan Tommy Douglas faced down the entrenched medical profession and brought in medicare.

These cultural, political, and social currents were not a conscious part of my decision to go back to *Saturday Night*, but they were the persuasive context in which, once the chance was offered, I never thought of not taking it.

And what of *Saturday Night*? What sort of business, what sort of organization was I taking over? It now had a demoralized skeleton staff, a dicey public image, and its advertising had hit rock bottom.

However, there were pluses compared with the Fengate venture. *Liberty* had gone. I had only acquired *Saturday Night*. I did not have to worry about circulation. Maclean Hunter had agreed to handle circulation at no net cost nor return. They would run our circulation fulfillment, collaborate with us on promotion, agree to maintain the current circulation level, and work hard to increase it. They would, in return, keep all circulation revenue and, more important, segregate our list from theirs. The man in charge would be Gordon Rumgay, the person who five years before had made the initial contact with me about *Saturday Night* as Jack Kent Cooke's general manager.

I also had no compunction in getting rid of Arthur Lowe, who had edited the *Canadian Saturday Night*, Bishop's merger of *The Canadian* and *Saturday Night*. He departed to edit a suburban weekly in Richmond Hill. Herbert McManus, the managing editor, also went to become the editor of an in-house magazine for the Anaconda Copper Company.

Only two people stayed on to my great relief and gratitude. In Toronto there was Reg Jeffs, the advertising representative and production manager who was nearing retirement and dedicated to *Saturday Night*. In Montreal there was Roy Tait, who was loyal to the point of self-immolation and had more contacts and good-will in the Montreal advertising and public relations fraternity than one would have thought possible in view of the gyrations of the magazine he represented.

Finally Bishop had made the magazine a monthly. So now I had three weeks to get out a first issue under the new regime.

Tait and Jeffs informed me that we had six and two-third pages of advertising committed only, so that there were thirty-four pages of editorial needed.

Peter Stursberg had continued as Ottawa editor through the *Canadian Saturday Night* period, so that took care of two pages. There were three pages of "Gold & Dross" material in hand. Mary Lowrey Ross had gone on writing beautifully all through the previous year, too. She had a lively review of Elizabeth Taylor's film *Cleopatra* on file.

Again friends rallied around. John Gellner was working on a piece as soon as he heard the announcement. Ken McNaught rang and asked what he could do. So did Nathan Cohen, then a very big name in Canada. And Arthur Hailey. Two other people had heard me announce the takeover on radio. David Levy came in and, after a half-hour discussion, became the new managing editor. Bill Nobleman, an advertising salesman, came in off the street straight from his car and found himself director of advertising. Trevor Hutchings, working at CFTO on set design, called in to ask whether he could be the art director, working at night.

An issue came together. Nathan Cohen wrote a review of Stratford as the cover story, and nothing could have surprised the right-wingers Bishop had put on the subscription list more than that. David Levy wrote a piece on Russia and China. (Levy spoke Russian and later became the CBC's correspondent in Moscow.) McNaught compared Lincoln and J. F. Kennedy. Gellner wrote on what he called "the start-and-stop, build-and-scrap, spur-of-the-moment" defence policies that had bedeviled the sixties. His final sentence echoed in my head all the way home after I had copyedited it: "One can but hope that this time we will at long last get something that is national, effective, and lasting." It was a good thought for the new *Saturday Night*.

We put the issue to bed, working several nights after 5:00 p.m. to accommodate Hutchings. These sessions were hardworking but often unconsciously hilarious. Rushing out of my office one night with galleys to pasteup, I asked why Levy was not pasting up what I had brought out before. Echoing a famous Dorothy Parker of the early days of *The New Yorker*, he said, quite unselfconsciously, "I can't. Hutchings has the brush."

There was hilarity, too, in choosing the pictures, especially those of Liz Taylor as Cleopatra and some burly bathing beauties for a piece on Australia's Great Barrier Reef.

("Shouldn't mind running on her reef." "I think she *is* the Great Barrier Reef." Sexist, inane, but at the end of a twelve-hour day working against the odds, it lightened us up a bit.)

Print day came, and we had made it. Then Seagram's pulled their outside back cover colour ad. "What do we do?" Ray Youngs, the printing foreman at Maclean Hunter, asked.

"Print it black," I said, "in mourning for lost advertising."

I never knew what grief printing a whole jet-black page would bring to the rest of the four-colour form. But with Ray at the mixing valves and me hovering at the receiving end, we got it passably right by 3:00 a.m. and put it to bed. Then I went to bed, as well.

A week later, on all the newsstands, the new *Saturday Night*, with Martha Henry on the cover, had this announcement inside:

> *As I was saying, before I was so rudely interrupted by* The Canadian, *this country needs a forum where the issues of the day can be debated with wit, intelligence, and responsibility. Saturday Night, back to its old and proud name, intends to provide that forum.*

The signed editorial ended:

> *This summer Canada is moving forward industrially. It is enjoying itself at Stratford and other festivals. It is waiting patiently for the time when Parliament goes on its holidays and the cabinet can get on with its job.*

> *But the fall will be a lively time politically and the winter may be bleak. Personally, with these columns once more available to me, I'm looking forward to whatever the future brings.*

> *Who wouldn't?*

Putting the issue together was easier than putting the organization back together. A board of directors was needed, and friends came to the rescue. (And indeed it was a rescue.) Jack Rhind, president of North American Life, came on. So did Lyman Henderson, president of Davis and Henderson. Jack Seed, the lawyer who had looked after my interests in the negotiations with Bishop, agreed to act as secretary.

The first two or three issues had good stuff in them, but the layout was amateurish. The organization of the material had not yet jelled. How could it, with one part-time and two full-time employees, not to mention my half-time involvement on editorial? Together with Bill Nobleman, I went to see all our old advertisers — and a lot of new ones. In Montreal I did the same with Roy Tait.

I had a suite in the Mount Royal Hotel and was there almost every Monday morning. Quebec then, as now, was volatile. In the February 1964 issue Stuart Keate wrote a letter to Roger Lemelin, asking in sophisticated terms what it was Quebec wanted. Lemelin's answer, a measured paean of praise for Quebec nationalism inside federalism, was masterly.

Letters poured in. Advertising was slower — most campaigns were then set at least for six months and often a year ahead. But our general marketing targets were realized. At the end of the first year we had attracted a lot of attention. The Keate-Lemelin correspondence had been widely commented on. Our editorial on the Kennedy assassination, plus an inspired cover for it by Trevor Hutchings, had also created a stir. An investigation of the conspiracy theory of that assassination by John Gellner was quoted in the press.

For November 1964 we had twenty-five pages of advertising, a sixty-page issue, a new managing editor, Harry Bruce, and articles or columns by Nathan Cohen, Peter Stursberg, Gordon Baker (editor of the *Canadian Churchman*), Philip Stratford, Arthur Hailey, Donald Gordon, William Nicholls, Mary Lowrey Ross, and Peter Gzowski.

I had also gotten a secretary who would become a warm

supporter of the effort, an ex-Australian named Laurie Laming. Her husband, Hugh Laming, was a news producer at the CBC. From him I got all the inside gossip about the turbulence surrounding the CBC's *This Hour Has Seven Days*. From her, for the next seven years, I got the most professional support, the warmest friendship, and most dedicated involvement a man could wish for. She also had a wicked sense of humour and a capacity for pricking pompous balloons that were a joy to listen to on the telephone.

Soon after she joined the staff, Personnel Placement Service asked me to participate in a secretaries' seminar. What did bosses expect? What did secretaries expect? What was the mix, et cetera.

I asked Laurie what she expected in her employer. In minutes she had the following memo on my desk:

Thoughts on the virtues and vices of my bosses, past and present

The cardinal sin of a lot of senior business executives is that they regard a highly efficient, well-paid secretary as a status symbol (that the prestige of their job requires it), and then, having hired her, proceed to treat her as a mentally deficient teenager.

I like to work for and with the man who:

- *treats me as an adult who has a brain in her head.*
- *combines wit with sagacity.*
- *doesn't breathe down my neck — metaphorically speaking — when I'm doing my job.*
- *expects good work for good pay.*
- *pays tribute to his secretary's intelligence by occasionally inviting her opinion on* other *as well as office matters.*
- *appreciates that employees do have private lives.*
- *avoids pomposity in speech and writing like the plague.*

- *is reasonably tidy in mind, and desk, and avoids* unnecessary *last-minute panics when he can.*
- *appreciates that punctuality is a virtue of princes.*
- *doesn't regard his secretary as a nagging shrew when she issues several reminders about an approaching deadline. (She's really acting as his own conscience in this!)*
- *who knows* he *is fallible, and above all, that* I *am, too.*

Despite this lengthy list I don't *look for perfection in the man I work for, as the perfect wife, the perfect secretary, and the perfect boss would merely add up to a boring bunch.*

I do *require my boss to like cats; I could never work successfully for a cat-hater.*

And finally, I say with Antony: "For I have neither wit, nor words, nor worth, / Action, nor utterance, nor power of speech, / To stir men's blood; I only speak right on; / I tell you that which you yourselves do know."

By the end of the first year Tish and I had also bought a house: a large but not grand place in Rosedale; had decided to keep our retreat on Garden Island near Kingston; and had settled in for what looked like a fascinating, rewarding and, doubtless, long haul to make *Saturday Night* what I had always wanted to make it — powerful and profitable.

XV

THE RESTLESS CHURCH

A FEW DAYS AFTER I HAD QUIT Bishop's *Saturday Night*, the Reverend Gordon Baker had asked me to lunch. "Now that you've quit working for *Saturday Night*," he said, "what about doing a bit for Sunday morning?" It was a jocular way of asking me to write a regular monthly column in the *Canadian Churchman*, the monthly paper of the Anglican Church in Canada, of which he was the innovative and energetic editor.

I had written the occasional article for him in the previous year or two, with results that had astonished me. I would write as pungently and persuasively as I could in *Saturday Night*, and one or at most two letter writers a month would respond. One article in the *Canadian Churchman* in 1960 had produced a dozen letters.

I was active in the Anglican Church. Brought up in an English village where the church, and the church school, were the centre of village life, I had early become involved. Our school holidays revolved around Christian feasts: Easter, Whitsun, Christmas, and the Harvest Festival. A window on the outside world in the days before television and radio was provided by Lenten lectures with slides. (Lantern slides, we called them, because the projector was an enormous affair — the slides over four inches square and made of glass.) I had been a choirboy, server, and choirman before I left home for university.

Only after very serious thought had I opted for an arts degree at Cambridge rather than priestly training at the college of the Sacred Mission at Kelham.

The war had diminished my faith. As Shakespeare wrote:

Few die well that die in battle. . . . Some swearing, some crying for a surgeon, some upon their wives left poor behind them, some upon the debts they owe, some upon their children rawly left.

I had seen such deaths, many of them, and my metaphysical stomach turned when our padre "blessed" our guns.

After the war, Albert Camus' and Jean-Paul Sartre's fictions based on Existentialism had intrigued me. I had read all their work at Cambridge just after the war, and in Canada my first article ever published was one on the Existentialist novels of Jean-Paul Sartre in the *Queen's Quarterly*.

But when we had children, something seemed lacking in the bare asceticism of Existentialism. The miracle of life, particularly after my wife had two very difficult births and almost died when our son was born, seemed to be just that. So back to the church and the Bible I went.

Tish had always been a confirmed believer, and as our family grew in Canada, we became involved parishioners, first at St. George's Cathedral in Kingston, then in Toronto at St. Simon-the-Apostle Church, Anglican parish church for Rosedale and St. Jamestown — a challenging mix.

Son Alastair had become a choirboy at St. George's, so he naturally became a choirboy at St. Simon's. His involvement took us more regularly and more often to church than either of us had been since our own childhood.

Because church worship should, in my view, be corporate worship, I had spoken out, both at St. George's and St. Simon's, about the choir's occasional takeover of the service as their own showcase. As in any voluntary society, once you have said what you feel ought to be done, you are inevitably asked to do it.

Tish soon became involved with the social assistance work of the parish, which included what is now St. Jamestown's apartment city. It was then a run-down, single-family slum, with the majority of people either unemployed or underemployed. Many were on welfare. Many were single parents. Long before most of society worried about such people, the church, as always, lent a helping hand.

There was also intellectual ferment in the church as a whole. The Roman Catholics were on the verge of Vatican II. Anglicans were reading *Honest to God*, a challenging, disturbing book by the English bishop of Woolwich. Dietrich Bonhoeffer's *Letters from Prison* was being widely circulated in paperback. And Anglicans, as a body, were going to meet in a great conclave — the Anglican Congress — in 1963 in Toronto.

It seemed a very good time to have a platform for one's views, so I said yes to Baker. I also said yes to George Snell, the suffragan bishop of Toronto, when he asked me, as a result of some things I had said at the Toronto Synod, to address a meeting of all the clergy at their diocesan meeting in Peterborough.

That meeting was to change our lives for the next ten years in one way and permanently in another. I began my talk by saying that, as a layman, I did not pretend to know the clergy side of the story. But I did feel that we were co-workers in the field, and I was "a fellow believer, though as yet imperfect in my belief." I pointed out all the things that were happening in society: more new churches being built than at any time since the nineteenth century; more coverage of church initiatives with young people; the "Christ in Christmas" campaign; and even grace-before-meal cards then appearing on restaurant tables.

I suggested that the church was now a more caring, more serving institution than it had been for some time, but I also asked that the leaders in the church, lay and clergy alike, should not just be active in picking up the broken members of society, but be prophetic in going after the institutions and people who broke them, especially unscrupulous employers, greedy developers, and venal politicians.

The Reverend John Thompson, rector of St. George's Willowdale, came up to me immediately after my talk, which had been well received, and asked, "Will you come and give such a talk in my church at the morning service? Give the sermon, in fact?"

That was a lot more difficult to say yes to.

The pulpit was the prerogative of the priest. I might say theologically unsound things. I might seem to be aping for twenty minutes those who had given their lives to the faith. On the other hand, I had been sincere in what I had said, and Thompson was sincere in following it up. He already had Bishop Snell's permission to offer me the pulpit.

If anything made me examine my motives, question my faith, that invitation did. I talked it over with Tish. "You have to do it," she said.

So, with trepidation, as nervous as a cat, and filled with a strong sense of unworthiness, I appeared at St. George's at 10:50 a.m. on the chosen Sunday. I would not wear cassock or surplice. Those I had relinquished when I left choir and sanctuary as server. I would, as John Thompson suggested, wear my academic gown and hood, as if I were giving a university lecture.

I assured him that, in agreeing, I would *not* give a lecture, either in matter or method, and certainly not in time. A phrase echoed from Gordon Baker's days at Wycliffe College: "For your sermon talk about God for about fifteen minutes."

Well, I did not talk so much about God, and I did go for (my wife later told me) some twenty minutes or more. But my plain talk about what Christians should do — that faithful body of men and women who constitute the body of Christ — seemed to strike a responsive chord.

I had had grave doubts about appearing in a pulpit. My whole upbringing had taught me to regard it almost as sacred as the altar.

(Just before her death I took my mother into the church where she had been baptized and confirmed at the beginning of the century. "No one is here," she said. "Do you think I could go up into the pulpit? I've always wanted to and never dared. But you go up now." So up *she* went, and came down with a beatific, satisfied smile on her face.)

I had also shied away from anything approaching a sort of Salvation Army sinners' bench confession. As our assistant curate had said one morning in *his* sermon, "Anglicanism is a quiet religion. Not too many Anglicans fall off their horse like St. Paul when he came to Christianity on the way to Damascus." Added to which, a clergyman friend had heard of my going to St. George's and said, "Well, you might do some good. But I'm wary of hit-and-run preachers."

And Dr. Johnson's famous remark about women preachers had haunted me. It "is like a dog's walking on his hinder legs. It is not done well; but you are surprised to find it done at all."

The comments as people came out of St. George's dispelled these fears. A layman had talked to them in their language. The rector, moreover, had had the courage to invite him. And the new perspective seemed to make people think.

Then the invitations came in thick and fast. In the short term, as I said, it changed our lives. For almost two years we were as often at someone else's church as our own. In one now unbelievable week in 1964 my diary reads:

Oct. 18 (Sunday) St. Hilda's, Oakville.
  19 St. George's-on-the-Hill, parish dinner.
  20 Grace Church: outreach committee talk.
  21 St. George's, in St. Catharines, parish dinner.

Working on Sunday morning, indeed, and by now on *Saturday Night*, as well.

These were the vintage years. I was just forty. We had a commodious house in Rosedale. Our children were growing up in all the ferment of the sixties, but seemed impervious to the grosser and more outrageous activities of some young people. They had hosts of friends who regularly came into the house.

"We can discuss *anything* in your house," one teenager said one day to me. "We never really talk to one another in ours."

It was a great compliment. For this was the age of the generation gap, when it was the accepted wisdom that no parents could possibly understand their children. Whether we understood them or not, we certainly talked to them. In our own family whoever got first hearing at dinner (always a formal sit-down with grace) relinquished it reluctantly. Arguments were fierce and noisy. Sarah, the youngest, sometimes had to wave her hand as if at school to get her turn. And judgements, even harsh ones, were made flatly.

"Why does Alastair take up so much time with his story about school and I'm not allowed time to tell mine?" Sarah asked on one notable occasion.

"Because your stories are boring," both older children replied in unison.

Sarah never forgot that — and it has made her the most amusing raconteur of the lot in later life.

Such family life was an enormous support for me and reflected on the superb job Tish had done with them. She was now heavily involved in volunteer work at the church and was already serving on the boards of various social service groups, ranging from Planned Parenthood, through Bloorview Hospital, to the metropolitan YWCA and the St. Christopher Settlement House.

When the United Church Women of Canada asked us to go out to their annual meeting at Banff, they wanted Tish to speak as well as me — and speak she did on how St. Simon's was coping with the blockbusting techniques of a vicious American developer in the slum to the south of the church. The developer was indeed stopped in his plans, and his successor, while erecting huge apartment blocks, was forced by pressure on the city council to provide park space and even two blocks of subsidized housing that the longtime residents of the demolished single-family dwellings could afford to move into.

Proof that one person, or one group of people, can change matters was St. Simon's involvement in the whole St. Jamestown saga. Not just socially for the people we were trying to help, but morally and ethically for the ones helping.

Example: we did a survey, through a trained parish worker, of the households we were helping with food and clothing. In several there was evidence that the children got knocked around when their parents were drunk. Yet there was love and family closeness the rest of the time. Did one put such children into the care of Children's Aid? Or did one leave them to have more love than they would get in a foster home at the price of a few tingling ears or spanked bottoms?

There was one case that made my secretary, Laurie Laming — who typed all the reports as *her* contribution — really stop dead in her typing. A brother and sister, both of cruelly low intellect and with physical deficiencies, too, were living as man and wife, with two children from the incestuous union, one of whom had a clubfoot. There was love and compassion and caring in this bizarre household. Should the laws of society break it up? Should these broken individuals be forced to give up what they did have? Or should the parish, should the priest, let sleeping dogs lie? What, in fact, would Jesus have done? Based on the accounts of the scriptures, he would heal them and tell them to sin no more. Without Jesus we tried to heal them first.

And this is where the long term of Gordon Baker's suggestion and Bishop Snell's invitation came in. Never had we, as a couple, investigated our faith so deeply. Never had we become more convinced that Thomas Carlyle had it right when he said, "Whatsoever thy hand findeth to do, do it with thy whole might."

So Tish organized and staffed a food and clothing exchange at the church. She brought fresh energy and vision to St. Christopher House where she sold the decrepit building they were in, built a new one, doubled the programme and the budget, and replaced half the directors with new, younger people. She also served as president of the St. Simon's Women's Auxiliary.

Furthermore, she became a part of a group of educated, intelligent, lively women who banded together to explore their faith. Affectionately known to their friends as the Godgirls, they were probing in their discussions and diligent in their reading.

I was shaken as I sat down to breakfast one morning when Tish asked, "Tell me, what do you think of the Holy Spirit?" It was not the sort of discussion we usually had at breakfast. Such discussion in the sixties was, however, much more evident everywhere. Bishop Robinson's *Honest to God* had made us all more honest to our faith. The "God is dead" remark echoed around. The war in Vietnam made even patriotism suspect and war a moral issue for the first time.

In Canada the Anglican Church commissioned Pierre Berton to write *The Comfortable Pew*, which not only gave good material for my speaking but, especially for services in the church, a wonderful opening. "Has anyone ever in any church found a comfortable pew? All are designed as penitents' benches, butting shrewdly into the kidneys if you try to relax, boring upwards through the buttocks if you sit straight."

From the Toronto Synod I was elected to the Provincial and General Synods. The General Synod nominated me to the Church and Society Conference of the World Council of Churches in Geneva in July 1966. That was an eye-opener for someone who had started out in a small village church in England and worshipped in a small city church now. Christians from all over the world came: Russian and Greek Orthodox; Coptic Christians from Egypt; Bar Toma Christians from India; Christians persecuted and attending at their peril from Africa, Asia, and Latin America.

I had been assigned to the section dealing with the Christian posture towards revolution, with an Indonesian, Mr. Taki Simatupang, as chairman. Wide-eyed as I was at the people around me, I found the same contentiousness as at the General Synod or parish council.

It took us almost a day to agree on the agenda. Then, when set speeches had been given, we were suddenly into drafting a report with very little time for discussion. The reports, too, being translated into five languages as they were presented, had necessarily to be simple in language. How could a nice nuance in English survive simultaneous translation into French, German, Russian, and Spanish?

Nevertheless, my professional pride as a writer could not allow some of the balder statements to be accepted as what we, in my section, had agreed on. My trips to the floor microphone were frequent, so when Margaret Mead (she of the pioneering work on sexuality in Samoa) rose to present her section report on Man and Community in Changing Societies, she asked that such nit-picking not be done on her report. The rapporteur's committee would straighten things out.

I could not, however, let one phrase go. In talking of the position of women in society she asked, "Are women to be comrades and partners of men, but not *under* them?" I suggested that the phrase might be more delicately put. The French, English, and Spanish roared with laughter. The Germans reinforced it when their translation caught up, and then the Russians, bobbing their priestly birettas, came last. The bishop of Delaware adjourned the session for coffee to restore proper seriousness to the rest of the report.

The whole conference was a mind-bending affair for me. Pastor Niemoller, who had faced down Hitler, was there. Martin Luther King addressed us by recording, the pulpit of the cathedral in Geneva empty as he spoke. Dom Helder Camara, the bishop of Recife, Brazil, who lived in an adobe hut outside his cathedral while his palace was given over to the homeless, was there. Barbara Ward, tireless advocate of the Third World, spoke, as did André Philip and Max Kohnstamm — legendary figures to me, both in the church and out of it.

We had had the same excitement during the Anglican World Congress in 1963 in Toronto where Barbara Ward had also been a speaker. That congress came alive from the very first speaker — Max Warren. "We do not, as Christians, have a monopoly on truth," he said. "In fact, in this century the two men who have so devastatingly laid open the ills of society and the ills of the individual soul are two Jews: Karl Marx and Sigmund Freud."

He was followed by Janet Lacey, who wondered, as she watched hollow-eyed children with protuberant, protein-starved bellies hunting in garbage in the slums of South America, who were the chosen people that the Prayer Book called on to be joyful. Who chose them? she asked.

In Geneva, in Toronto, in our own parish, these things were being discussed as they never had been before. I was asked to discuss them as speaker at the Diocesan Synod of Huron; at the social services committee annual meeting of the diocese of Nova Scotia in Halifax; at the Synod of Caledonia in Kitimat, a town much enlarged since Tish and I had visited it in 1956; at Seabury House, the national centre of the Episcopalian Church of the United States; and at the Synod in Calgary. I talked of these things and the ideas put forward to graduating theological students in Toronto, London (Ontario), and Saskatoon.

I was asked to co-chair a follow-up conference in Montreal on the problems of poverty in Canada. The speakers were Dom Helder Camara; Madame Vanier, wife of the then governor-general of Canada; and a Princeton University professor, Richard Schull, who had had extended mission experience in South America. Just as I was introducing the speakers, the doors burst open on both sides of the stage and two columns of Montreal East Enders came in, bearing placards saying We Are the Poor. The leader grabbed the microphone, and my French was not up to understanding his demotic joual.

Then something special happened. Madame Vanier took the microphone, and in her perfect French answered the man's questions. Then Bishop Camara took the microphone and asked them all to meet him outside. In the large foyer of the University of Montreal building where we were meeting, he spoke through a bullhorn.

"My brothers and sisters," he said, "we are trying to help you — to help poor people everywhere. Jesus told us to do that. You know He did. But we cannot do it if you stop our meeting. Do not disrupt us. Pray for us. Please, let us all pray."

Every one of the protesters sank to their knees and prayed with him, then left us silently as they would leave church after mass.

Camara is the nearest thing to a modern-day saint I have ever met, and I have been privileged to meet him several times. The last time he was on a visit to Canada to raise money for his people. The lunch was for a high-powered group of Canadian businessmen doing business in Brazil. As he came into the private dining room at the National Club, he saw me, came over, embraced me, and said, "My brother." I could have wept. Such a humble man with such a powerful presence, founded on a rock-solid faith and a shining example of works. Wherever he spoke I always felt he was on his way to heaven, and if we tried, we could be part of the company. But it would mean dedication, fearlessness, and a passionate faith.

The Christian community worldwide is not as active now. Pope John Paul II has stopped reform — or at least the reforms of Pope John XXIII evolved at Vatican II — in its tracks. The Anglican communion has lacked leadership and conviction in recent years. But what we all sought and prayed for so earnestly in the sixties has, in fact, come partly to pass, and the torch has been passed on to many secular groups and, in recent times, to rock singers like Bob Geldof.

My columns in the *Canadian Churchman* changed, at the wish of the new editor, from a general column to one on the arts in 1973. In 1990 it was discontinued altogether, the General Synod committee responsible for the newspaper having asked the acting editor to concentrate more on theological and ecclesiastical matters and dispense with all columns by the laity.

What has happened, I suppose, is that the lay energy of the sixties and seventies has grown less as that generation has grown older. A new society, more intent on other issues — the environment, AIDS, waste disposal, global ecology — operates outside the church.

The church, therefore, concerns itself with more churchly things: liturgy, the language of the Prayer Book, the restructuring of its own organization to cope with increased urbanization, and the gradual emptying of hundreds of rural communities.

It is a long way from *Honest to God, The Comfortable Pew*, and the days when St. Simon's not only forced a developer to change his plan, but got me onto the city planning board to see that the change was carried out. But I am still grateful — maybe eternally grateful — to all those clergy, Bishop Snell, Bishop Wilkinson, Archbishop Hambidge, Gordon Baker, George Birch of Metropolitan United Church, Archbishop Pocock of the Roman Catholic Diocese, and many others, who inspired and directed my return to the committed Christian fold.

All of the decade came together in my book, *Some Camel, Some Needle*, which was published in 1974. Its preface still echoes what the decade from 1964 to 1974 did — and still does — for me personally:

> *[This book] is my own celebration of a faith which, despite its darker moments, has been a constant source of excitement to me, spiritually, intellectually, and aesthetically.*

> *I cannot praise a cloistered virtue. I cannot accept a solemn religion. But a faith whose founder could turn water into wine to make a wedding swing is a liberating, joyous, exciting faith. So throughout my life it has proved.*

XVI

A HARD — AND
WRONG — DECISION

THE AUGUST 1965 ISSUE OF *Saturday Night* carried this note on its masthead page:

Anniversary: Two years ago this month the first issue of the new Saturday Night *was being put to bed by the editor and one half-time art man. This month we start our third year with a full staff. Kildare Dobbs is managing editor, fresh from a year in Spain where he rested on the somewhat financially thin laurels of a Canada Council Senior Arts Fellowship. The former half-time art man, Trevor Hutchings, is now our full-time and very inventive cover designer and layout man. Arnold Edinborough is still the editor.*

We also have a staff of a dozen contributing editors in New York, Vancouver, London, England, and other glamorous places writing on the whole gamut of human affairs.

Two years ago we had no money and, some thought, no prospects. We have now moved into the black, we are glad to say — and will be publishing in the coming months the fattest fall issues this publication has ever put out.

It was a puff piece. But it was true. Since that momentous August issue of 1963, with its black back cover and its arrogant editorial note, we really had come a long way.

Trevor Hutchings, with covers I still see with pleasure when leafing through bound copies of the magazine, had given us good visibility on the newsstands. Inside we were a little amateurish and inconsistent, but the layout was always germane and usually attractive.

David Levy, the first managing editor of the new regime, had worked hard at it and, when he left to be the CBC's correspondent in Moscow, Harry Bruce had filled the gap with great professionalism. Harry was a quiet man with a wry but highly developed sense of humour. His father, Charles Bruce, had run Canadian Press and been a well-regarded poet.

Though Harry had grown up in Toronto, he was a Maritimer at heart and has for many years now gone back to live in "the old Bruce place" in Nova Scotia. Nevertheless, he knew Toronto as a city like the back of his hand and, in the persona of Max Macpherson, had written in the *Toronto Star* about his engaging walks in its byways and back alleys.

He had come to a magazine in which some of the regular writers were friends of mine who wanted to support what they probably felt was a mad, quixotic venture.

Nathan Cohen, fearsome drama critic and entertainment editor of the *Toronto Star*, wrote a monthly column, "In View." As the chairman of the CBC's most-watched Sunday programme, *Fighting Words*, he had inside knowledge of the CBC, of its fratricidal politics between producers, of its bureaucratic stumbling in programming, of its engorged technical staff. This made his column in *Saturday Night* essential reading for all broadcast people, both those on the inside and those who were trying to get there.

Cohen was devastating in his criticisms of the pretensions of early Toronto theatre. "One way for a Toronto drama critic to find good Canadian acting is to leave Toronto," he wrote in February 1965. He did not like the "great artistic director" attitude. "Of all the sins to be placed at the feet of Sir Tyrone Guthrie so far as Canada is concerned, the worst is his propagation, by example, of the führer principle," he wrote in June that same year.

William Nicholls, head of religious studies at UBC, was writing regularly on the ferment in the church. Reviewing a book of essays by leading Roman Catholics — *Objections to Roman Catholicism* — he shocked many readers by quoting one pungent paragraph by Magdalene Goffin, daughter of E. I. Watham, a famous and conservative Catholic historian.

There was nothing conservative in what Nicholls quoted from *her* writing: "In the same sense that the Jews made gods of their bellies by inventing an elaborate food code, so Roman theologians have made gods of the human reproductive organs. . . . If the Americans had dropped thousands of contraceptives over Japan instead of bombs that merely killed, maimed, and shrivelled up thousands alive, there would have been a squeal of outraged protest from the Vatican to the remotest mass centre in Alaska."

I had met Nicholls while visiting at UBC in the gap year between Bishop's takeover and mine.

I had known Kenneth McNaught, professor of history at the University of Toronto, on Garden Island for years. He wrote penetratingly on national affairs with a left leaning, while John Gellner wrote on international and military affairs from a rightist tilt as he covered the war in Vietnam.

Bruce knew a new generation of writers — not academic — and through him we now had Peter Gzowski writing on sports, Robert Fulford on films, Jack Batten on jazz, Harry Malcolmson on art, and Donald Gordon on the press. Together with Mary Lowrey Ross, still sturdily pecking away at the inanities of sixties television, and Peter Stursberg, covering Ottawa, knowing everyone *and* their history, it was a good stable of writers.

Partly it reflected the muddle at *Maclean's* magazine, where editors and managing editors came and went all through the 1960s. Without Ralph Allen and Pierre Berton *Maclean's* was a rudderless, inconsequential magazine without flair and without focus, despite the efforts of people like Ken Lefoli and Charles Templeton. Writers looking for a platform would sooner come to *Saturday Night* with its smaller circulation but higher standards, even at lower cost. None of our writers was paid more than $100 for an article, less sometimes for a column.

Kildare Dobbs took over as managing editor from Harry Bruce. He had a lot going for him; and by his coming, we had a lot going for *Saturday Night*.

For the next three years I felt *Saturday Night* did what I had desperately wanted it to do. It contained some of the liveliest writing on contemporary affairs in the country. It covered the Vietnam War as well as student revolt, and its major piece on the centennial was by D. G. Creighton, the dean of Canadian historians. It chose Pierre Trudeau as the new Liberal leader before he had agreed to let his name stand (and I waited out his acceptance as a hundred thousand copies of the magazine were being printed — useless if he demurred and catastrophic to our tight budget).

The conditions of working were pleasant. Our staff was concentrated in a corner of an old but well-maintained building next to the Royal York Hotel, where I spoke so often that at lunch I was always brought fruit and at dinner rare roast beef whatever the menu of the convention or club I was addressing.

Reg Jeffs, the only man who had survived since the Consolidated Press era, before even Jack Kent Cooke, was the quiet, grateful coordinator of advertising. Jack Wilson, a devout Catholic, was advertising manager, his influence such that when his daughter underwent life-threatening surgery, the whole office prayed for its success (and it succeeded). Bill Nobleman, the general manager who had been elected to the Scarborough Board of Education by one vote over his opponent, went energetically and optimistically about getting major advertising contracts. A trip anywhere — to the next block, the next province, or the next country — would have him back in the office afterwards saying, "I shall be bitterly disappointed if we do not get twelve pages from Corby's," or General Motors, or whoever. He *was* often disappointed, but he never let it show. He was always promising the next raft of luscious four-colour advertising.

All together in one space, there was none of that editorial snobbery towards advertising that kept, in its early days, *The New Yorker* ad staff on another floor from the editorial.

We all knew we were head over heels into making *Saturday Night* work. An article that caused a stir, like the exchange of letters between Roger Lemelin from Quebec and Stuart Keate from Vancouver, was as exulted in by the advertising crew as it was by the editorial side. The recapture of double-page spreads from the automotive industry for its new models was welcomed by the editorial side because it gave us colour to work with in the editorial pages.

And the paragraph in the August issue had been true: in October we had double-page spreads for Ford's middle-size cars and for Thunderbird and Lincoln Continental; in November we had similar riches from GM for Chevrolet, Buick, and Cadillac, followed by Pontiac in December.

The issues were sixty-four and eighty-four pages, with writing by Jean Ethier-Blais, George Johnston, Jocelyn Dingman, Wendy Michener, and Jeannine Locke, as well as Kildare Dobbs himself and our usual group of commentators.

One contributor was a shot in the dark. I read the *Village Voice* regularly as an antidote to the *New York Times* and had been impressed by columns written by David McReynolds. I wrote him out of the blue and asked him to write on American affairs, an area of even greater interest in the sixties because of Vietnam and the draft-dodgers. He turned out to be the general secretary of the War Resisters' International League, a tall rangy guy in denims with a shoulder bag. We could not have found a more apt person for those polarized years.

Every so often we would have a contributing editors' dinner and general gabfest. Held at the staid Albany Club, they were evenings of intense intellectual excitement for me, plus a certain nervous feeling with McReynolds, Gellner, Dobbs, McNaught, Stursberg, and others all in one room. They were a mixed bunch, but their craftsmanship, their experience, their knowledge, and their enthusiasm were a tonic.

Dobbs was a delight to work with. He invented weird ideas: a picture spread featuring a nude model imposed on Harold Town paintings for a Valentine's Day issue (Town and the model got on famously, and she did not leave the studio for two days); another pictorial featuring the prison sketches of Gershon Iskowitz; a portfolio of photographs by Lutz Dille.

Kildare invented and ran a short story contest, sponsored by Belmont cigarettes, which was won by Austin Clarke, then a relatively newly arrived writer from the Caribbean. He also persuaded people writing for other magazines and newspapers to use pseudonyms so that they could write for us. The *Toronto Star* had decreed that no *Star* writer should write for *Saturday Night*. So we lost Nathan Cohen. But Robert Fulford became Marshall Delaney for years after, Brad Russell was Jack Batten, and Cameron Darby was Alexander Ross. All these men were then young and on the way up. We were the beneficiaries of their energy, vitality, and desire to speak in their own voice if not in their own name.

We were a happy, hardworking bunch, but there was wit and humour in the office. There was real family feeling then, and the downtown Toronto of those days was not the glass curtain-walled fortress it is now, with most of its pedestrian life under the streets in endless ill-signed concourses. We had a choice of the Royal York, the Walker House, the Prince George, and the Lord Simcoe for lunch, as well as Winfields — a smoked meat place run by a large, balding, somewhat irascible man who cut the meat, made the cash, bawled out the waitresses, and greeted all his regulars by name. His was a winter place just a block up from the office. A walk in arctic air got you hungry. The steamy deli smell welcomed you, and the soups were hearty — navy bean, chili, tomato and rice, beef broth, and chicken gumbo full of fresh rich okra. The special (it was Harry's special every day — it never changed because it *was* so special) was smoked meat on rye with french fries, tangy pickles and, for me always, a side order of pickled green tomatoes. All of this was served in thick stoneware china on Formica tables by harassed but friendly waitresses, and its price level nowadays is served from a counter in plastic cups and on paper plates with throwaway spoons and forks.

Winfields was even more popular in the sixties than Winston's, where Oscar Bercelleur's business was quietly dying, its grandeur faded, its theatre clientele long gone, its erratic standards quite unworthy of its price.

For lunches with conversation there were two places. One was the Captain's Table in the Lord Simcoe, whose flossy Pump Room had long since been closed. In the Captain's Table there was a round corner table that just seated the editorial group — Trevor Hutchings, Kildare Dobbs, Laurie Laming, and myself, plus one or two such as John Gellner or Ken McNaught, and where many a forward plan was evolved, again with good service and reasonable prices. There was a great haunch of beef hanging from a hook for those who wanted dinner midday, and a tempting smorgasbord for those who had dinner to go home to.

The other special place was a favourite of Bill Nobleman's — the Embers Room at the Prince George, where stuffed jumbo shrimps would have Bill's estimate of promised advertising leaping upwards, even if afterwards and in the cold light of his office, he proved to be bitterly disappointed.

Laurie and I, just the two of us, would also go to the Swiss Bear in the Walker House where, particularly in the fall, we enjoyed a plate of oysters and a salad. Very palatable and very slimming, for it takes as much energy to eat an oyster as it contains.

All around us were smallish stores, many of which catered to the garment people who inhabited most of the rest of our building at 55 York Street. These garment people were friendly folk, and on several occasions I found myself at cocktail parties and evenings as a guest, surrounded by fashion models. What was nice about those invitations was that they did not expect an article or mention in *Saturday Night* afterwards. Most other PR gatherings did. But the garment people knew we did not cover their industry, either from a business or design point of view.

There was a cigar store, a tailor, a secondhand bookshop, the *Star*, the *Globe and Mail*, all within a five-minute walk. And the subway was only ten steps outside our building's front door — and a bank in the street-level corner of the building itself.

Working downtown in later years was never as intimate, as people-conscious, as it was then. And as for lunch, there is now only one choice — plastic or price.

With such a staff, on which I absolutely relied, and with such a working atmosphere, it made it easy for me to do the travelling across the country that I thought was the easiest and cheapest public relations for the magazine.

Church groups — diocesan meetings rather than parish services — invited me. So did teachers. And the Canadian Club was keen to mount marathon journeys, such as the two in 1964 that took me, between April 20 and May 1, to Revelstoke, Kamloops, Vernon, Kelowna, Penticton, Comox-Port Alberni, and Victoria in British Columbia, with Edmonton, Calgary, and

Winnipeg on the way home and, in November, to Fredericton, Moncton, Saint John, St. Stephen, Halifax, and Charlottetown.

Everywhere in these places, because of *Fighting Words*, I was asked to do interviews on the local radio or television station. Everywhere I plugged away at *Saturday Night* and, in the hotels, took it from the back of the newsstand and put it prominently in the front row.

It was all a great expense of energy, but teachers, Canadian Clubbers, and church people *did* read. A special mailing to clergy of the Anglican Church netted us an 8 percent return, most of it with cash enclosed. A general mailing was reckoned worth it at between 1.8 and 2 percent.

This activity could only be sustained by a solid staff at the office and, more important, an understanding, loyal family who not only went serenely on through school, but did not get involved in all the sixties promiscuous, drug-experimenting, and Woodstock-style sex.

We took our own trips, too. In 1964 we took the March break down to North Carolina, where we found a warm welcome from friends, but where an unseasonable cold snap made the blossoms shake against the cold. It did not deter us, though, from investigating Gettysburg with its great diorama, the elegant restoration of Williamsburg, and the wide-sweeping spaces of Washington, D.C.

There was one tricky moment. Watching the final battle of the Civil War, with me sitting next to a huge, three-hundred-pound Southerner, Sarah (aged eight) leaned towards me and asked, "Which are the good guys?" — a question in those circumstances not to be asked.

She had a relatively successful first trip by car. She slept full-length in the back of the station wagon, encouraged to do so by her two older siblings, who wanted the back seat to themselves. Years later we found out that she had done so for a more urgent reason: if we crashed, she did not want to see it. Just wake up dead, she said, when it was all over.

March break 1964 was followed by a Maritime camping trip in the summer of 1965, where Mavor Moore, artistic director of the Charlottetown Summer Festival's second year, had chairs put into a sold-out house for us all to see *Anne of Green Gables*. We also stayed with friends on the French River in Nova Scotia and camped in Cape Breton, where a one-armed farmer quoted a price of two dollars for the night. We showed surprise at such a modest sum. Misinterpreting my exclamation, he quickly asked, "Is that too much for you, sir, with your family and all?"

In late August we camped above Edmundston, and there was a thin sheet of ice on the water bucket outside the tent. That meant it was time to go home — down the valley, into Rivière-du-Loup, one of the most spectacular views in the country, a short stay in Quebec City, where the weather was still warm and both daughters bought paintings from the street artists which, I notice, despite their later sophistication, still hang in their houses. And so home up the St. Lawrence, all three (a nine-year-old sitting up, not asleep, not worried any longer about a crash) singing softly from *Anne of Green Gables*: "Where has the summer gone to?"

Apart from a trip to Expo in 1967, it was the last shared external family holiday. Garden Island was *always* there every summer. But in 1966 Tish and I decided that after three gruelling years for me at *Saturday Night*, crossing and recrossing the country, talking to wholesale magazine distributors, advertising agents, potential ad accounts, as well as a variety of audiences, and for her bringing up the family single-handedly, we should have some time together away from it all.

So, with a little help from the Italian Tourist Board and Alitalia in organizing it, we set off to spend most of June and July in Italy. I had spent two years and more in Italy during the war, having landed at Salerno and gone, mostly on foot, all the way to Trieste.

I knew the country well. Both of us had seen a lot of Italian art outside the country, especially in Britain. It would be warm, and I could speak enough Italian, remembered from the war years, to order a meal or a bed and ask directions with a reasonable chance of understanding the answer.

The trip was more than we had ever imagined. The weather was good — sun every day. The roads were not clogged, as they are in these past summers. We only booked hotels ahead in three places: Rome, Florence, and Venice.

Images of that holiday recur constantly.

The afternoon we woke up in Venice to shouting outside our late-siesta window and saw a gondola race — a race for Italians, not tourists. The day we spent in Siena watching the whole lead-up to the *palio* and the struggle to get out of the square just before the final race. Tish lost almost every button on her blouse jostling her way out of the square, not through pawing hands, but sheer pressure of people.

The late golden morning we arrived in Fiesole and found the Della Robbia Museum closed. Persistent ringing produced an elderly curator. I explained in careful Italian what a disappointment for my wife it would be if, after my discovery of it during the war and singing its praises, she could not see it. He opened the door for us, locked it behind us, took us to each piece, commented on it in Italian, and waited for me to translate it for her. The evening in Vicenza where we attended a performance for the local theatregoers of Shakespeare's *Richard II* (*Ricardo Secundo*) and heard John of Gaunt thunder forth, "*Quella terra, quella bella terra, quella Inghilterra!*"

At Stresa we took the large suite over the central door of the Grand Hotel et des Iles Borromees, which had two double beds, a dressing room with bath for each of us, and breakfast for $50 U.S.

Those were the days when the going was good. Even grand

hotels, the Due Turri in Vicenza, the Grand et des Iles Borromees in Stresa, the Tritone in Praiano, and the Albergo Cappucini in Amalfi, were open for casual business at modest rates in June, gave excellent service, and even suggested, as the concierge did at the Brufani in Perugia, where we should dine out of the hotel.

The Brufani was one wonderful link back to the grimmer days of the war. I had asked for the corner room on the third floor that looked northward over the Umbrian hills. The concierge, over-hearing, asked if I had been there before since I was so specific. "Yes," I said, "as a captain on leave during 1944."

When we returned from dinner that evening, he called me over. There was the 1944 registration book with my signature: "T240494 Capt. A. Edinborough, R.A."

The other notable occasion was in Rome. I had several times been invited to the restaurant, Ranieri's, by members of the Ricasoli family after we liberated their Castel di Brolio, the heart of the Chianti country. The restaurant was, in fact, off-limits to Allied personnel, and reserved for Italians in 1944-45.

George and Jane Sinclair had, by chance, met us on the way to Italy, and the four of us agreed to revisit Ranieri's. When we arrived, the now elderly maître d' took a closer look at me and then, with much pumping of the hand and a light embrace, said: *"Benvenuto di nuovo, Barbuto Capitano Inglese."* (I had grown a beard since army days.) *"Ah, mi scusi, un più grasso, ma va bene cosi, Capitano Inglese."* He was right: I was fatter, but it was a great moment.

There were many more before we finally drove through the Simplon Pass into Switzerland to stay at the same little hotel in Crans-sur-Sierre where we had spent a delayed honeymoon in 1946. But the little mountain village we had known was now a huge, apartment-blocked resort full of German and Belgian tour-ists. And so we moved on to Geneva, where I registered at the World Council of Churches conference and Tish flew to London.

We were youngish, we had enthusiasm, we had a modest amount of money, and we had a magical holiday month — meeting the summer crowd only briefly in Venice. Only on two occasions did we deliberately revisit war sites: Cassino, where I paid my respects to six members of my artillery troop who lie still in the cemetery there, and Bibbiena, where an Italian family with a pretty daughter made me welcome anytime I could get there.

"I'm a nice wife to come back with you to an old girlfriend's place," Tish said.

"I'm a nice husband to bring you," I said, and we drove into the Pass of Muraglioni with our own thoughts.

Our son wrote a letter from his summer camp on Georgian Bay, which was waiting for us in Geneva. "I hope you are having a wonderful time reliving old memories and storing up new ones." No one could have said it better.

But by the time Expo 67 was over and the centennial was fading, Saturday Night Publications was running into trouble.

We had started a magazine for teachers entitled, cutely enough, *Monday Morning*. We wanted, we said, to give help and encouragement to our teachers. And when better to offer it than Monday morning?

Nobleman was a school trustee, and Jack Wilson was involved in part-time community college teaching. I had spoken to every English-speaking (and one Francophone) provincial teachers' group in the country. Bruce Mickleburgh, a sturdy NDP teacher and organizer with a large network of friends in the profession, became editor, and people like Eric McLuhan, Wilfrid Weese, and John McMurtry were eager to write for us. Northrop Frye did a long interview.

We needed more capital than we had. The original mailing of a hundred and fifty thousand copies reaped four thousand subscriptions, which our computer company promptly put on file, then lost.

Maclean Hunter, with a bill for printing still unpaid from 1964 (by original agreement), was edgy. David Fry, who had put over $300,000 into the venture, was running out of luck and money. (He lost his money and his registration as a broker the same week his mother died.) And Kildare Dobbs, having served valiantly, wanted more time to write rather than edit other people's copy, so he had quit a year earlier. Now Jack Batten, who had stepped in, also resigned.

The word went out that *Saturday Night* needed a new managing editor, and Robert Fulford walked in. "I have come," he said, "with a preposterous suggestion. I do not wish to be managing editor. I wish to be editor."

I thought about it. *Monday Morning* was in trouble. We had also bought a magazine in Quebec founded by Peter Desbarats, *Parallele*, and were issuing it in French quarterly, with articles translated from *Saturday Night*. Conversely *Saturday Night* carried articles by Michel Roy, Robert Bourassa, Norbert Lacoste, and Mario Cardinal translated into English.

Saturday Night itself was sound. Our stable of writers now included Christina Newman from Ottawa and Sir Peter Kirk from England. The advertising in place for the September and October issues was solid and plentiful. Maybe, I thought, I should concentrate more on the business side and more on *Parallele* and *Monday Morning*.

That same day the deal was struck. Fulford would inherit the job that I had always wanted, had gone through a roller-coaster series of ownerships to get, and had worked endlessly to keep. It was a hard decision.

In the end it was the wrong decision. Not to hire Fulford, but to think I could have the revivifying effect on the business side as I had undoubtedly had on the editorial side of Saturday Night Publications Limited.

I now haunted ad agencies with Bill Nobleman on behalf of

Monday Morning. I found a staunch ally in Floyd Chalmers, who from his chairman's position twice stopped Donald Campbell, the new chief executive officer of Maclean Hunter, from pulling the rug from under us. I talked to people with money who might take up where David Fry, now out of business and penniless (not, however, all due to his involvement with *Saturday Night*), had been forced to leave off.

And why did I do this? Because I believed in Canada. Its constantly changing and evolving attitudes were models for other countries. From an essentially farming and mining community it had changed, through war and peace, into an industrial, technologically driven one. Yet its burgeoning cities were not trashed by unscrupulous development, nor by slums allowed to rot in the centre while suburbs formed a concrete ring around them. Quebec particularly had come through a Quiet Revolution that had broken the power of an alliance between a reactionary church and big business. Vast numbers of immigrants had been allowed, through various multicultural initiatives at both provincial and federal level, to keep their own traditions while accepting a new kind of society. We had shown compassion to those thousands of Americans who had fled the draft for what they honestly believed to be an unjust, unethical, and unnecessary war. Our own forces were deployed in Cyprus and Palestine as peacekeepers, and doing a solid, honest job of it. I had seen their reputation firsthand in both Cyprus and Israel.

The creative arts had been fostered by the Canada Council and private enterprise to a point inconceivable when I had come to Canada. When I went to London on business in the sixties, I did not feel that I had to go to theatre, opera, and ballet because I was denied it at home.

There were strong, if yet young, opera companies in six cities, and three superb ballet companies, each reflecting, in Winnipeg, Toronto, and Montreal respectively, their own growing style and tradition. We had had two intellectually acute prime ministers in succession, Pearson and Trudeau. The centennial celebrations had been of a quality and quantity that had astonished ourselves as much as the world who came, in their millions, to share them.

There were problems. We were overgoverned. Our provincial education systems, each directed by a swollen, theoretical bureaucracy, had used the baby-boomers to invent ways of wasting millions of dollars on empire-building and untried pedagogic experiments. There were sinister elements attempting to take over Quebec's Quiet Revolution and to heat it up after Che Guevara's model in Cuba. There was a widening split between eastern factories, propped up in protected inefficiencies, and western farming and mining, whose tools had been rendered more expensive by national policy when their product was losing its value through international competition.

A voice — many voices — were needed to counter the difficulties and keep the excitement and pride of the centennial going. That was my motive in keeping *Saturday Night* strong. But nobody with money wanted to hear. This year's bottom line blocked out the next generation's Canada.

After leading a trip to the South Seas as an advertising gimmick for *Saturday Night*, I called the directors — Nobleman, Fry, Seed — together and said that I could see no future. I had put a mortgage on my house to pay the salaries one week. I had not taken a salary on other paydays. The company was bankrupt.

Fry and Nobleman, however, would not agree. "As long as we have a company," Fry said, "we have a chance."

So I offered my shares — a controlling seventy percent interest — to them both at a negligible amount, asked for assurances that my debts owing from the company would be paid, and resigned all active participation in a venture that had been my whole exciting, rewarding life for ten years. It meant a savage retrenchment for me personally, and the sale of my house, I knew, would be needed to cover those *Saturday Night* loans I had personally guaranteed.

It was hardest for Bob Fulford, only a year into the job, though Fry and Nobleman were both hit hard. Fry had lost everything. Nobleman had an editor he did not yet know and two publications he had to kill: *Monday Morning* and the French *Parallele*.

One early December morning in 1969 I arrived home. "I have no magazine, mounting debts, no money, and no job," I said.

"Happy Christmas," Tish replied.

XVII

AN ARTS MISSION

D AVID FRY WAS RIGHT. EVEN THE shell of a company can be worth something, and though *Saturday Night* closed down temporarily after I left it, Nobleman and Fulford did resurrect it, and it has survived to grace another Canadian day.

A group of wealthy people "saved" it, first under the general urging of Arthur Gelber. Then Norman Webster, a highly competent journalist from a wealthy family, took it on. Conrad Black, a man with a passion for print and a very deep pocket, which some of that print (notably England's *Daily Telegraph*) helps to fill, bought it from Webster. But with a staff of a dozen or so, an editorial budget that may spend more for one article than I did for a whole issue, it still, I note, has less advertising per issue than the ones we put out in those exhilarating sixties.

The problem with *Saturday Night* — and more particularly with *Monday Morning* — was always money. Now that I had walked away from them, it was my problem. My house had a third mortgage on it, which had been all spent in one month in 1969 to pay the wage bill. A personal friend — a widow at that — was owed $25,000 on my signature and that of David Fry. Fry was out of funds so it all devolved on me.

I had some long-term plans, but I needed short-term money. I asked Paul Deacon, the editor of *The Financial Post* and a very good friend, if he could see me the day after I had signed over my *Saturday Night* stock. No one as yet knew that I had done so, outside *Saturday Night's* directors.

"Wouldn't a column about the arts," I said to Paul, "which was aimed at the businessmen who give money to them and serve on their boards, be a good thing for *The Financial Post*?"

"Yes, it would," he said, "but who could write it?"

"I could."

"Yes, you could."

"Well, that's why I'm here. I have just resigned from *Saturday Night*, sold my shares, shouldered the debt, and am unemployed."

"You've got the column," he said. "Twice a month to begin with." Then, and only then, when business had been dealt with, did he commiserate about *Saturday Night*.

That was touching. I had the job before the commiseration. He wanted the column for itself, not because I needed the money.

The mandate was simple. Anything about the arts, or what is now called "lifestyle," including food, travel, wine, and books.

I mentioned that I could not write about the arts for a national newspaper from Toronto alone. I did get around the country quite a bit for speaking engagements, so a modest travel budget and some creative planning would get the *Post* nationwide, if selective, coverage at a bargain rate.

This was agreed upon. The price per column, its length, and how it would be handled in the office was also spelled out.

Within half an hour, and with a half sheet of notepaper outlining the bare facts of our agreement, I shook hands with Paul. So began a twenty-year association with a group of newspaper professionals that was, from start to finish and through three editors, a delight. No one ever had better support, or a better pulpit from which to persuade the business and arts communities that there is creativity, daring, dedication, and hard work in both; that, in fact, once the stereotypes are down, that each can learn from the other and both can share in the satisfaction of a commitment honoured and a job well-done.

Looking back, it is interesting to me that I did not, this final time of leaving *Saturday Night*, even glance at universities. Simon Fraser University in Burnaby, British Columbia, had, late in the sixties, asked me to become its vice president, hoping that my communications skills might help its troubled image outside and its faculty-student strife inside. An approach was also made by a member of the search committee for a new president for Bishop's University in Lennoxville, Quebec. A tentative (and, as far as I know, totally unauthorized) approach was made by a board member of King's College, Halifax.

But the only president of a university who will be respected by his faculty is one who has academic credentials. Teaching and learning are what universities are all about. Fund-raising, student recruiting, and corporate and government relations are all part of university administration, but lesser people in lesser jobs than that of president can be hired to do those things. The president should be academically distinguished. I was not, and so did not pursue any of these leads, even though I spent two enlightening days at Simon Fraser with board, staff, and students at the height of the student radical movement there.

Journalism was now my craft. Speaking on television, radio, and the public platform was my avocation. Thomas Carlyle again: "Produce! Produce! Were it but the pitifullest infinitesimal fraction of a Product, produce it, in God's name. . . . Up, up! Whatsoever thy hand findeth to do, do it with thy whole might. Work while it is called Today; for the Night cometh." So, for the next three years, that is exactly what I did: not because the Night was coming, though it might well, but because I had debts to pay, a family to support, and the creditors were coming.

Not long into my writing career for the *Post* came one of those breaks that change one's life. I had written a column about the ubiquitous presence of Rothman's in the performing and visual arts. There was not a major summer festival that did not have a Rothman's-sponsored souvenir programme. There was not a major art gallery that did not have some time set aside each year for a large touring exhibition of international art initiated and paid for by Rothman's. In Stratford, Ontario, the art gallery was the Rothman's Gallery. An imaginative rehabilitation of the old waterworks, the gallery's reconstruction had been a centennial project for Rothman's, which then gave a substantial annual sum for its staffing and programming year-round, a year that always launched the new Rothman's exhibition at the same time as the festival opened.

In all this activity Rothman's of Pall Mall Canada Limited was doing, in a Canadian context, what Anton Rupert, the South African chairman of Rothman's parent, the Rembrandt Tobacco Company, insisted all his subsidiaries do. In Holland the Turmac Tobacco Company had commissioned fifteen major European artists to each do a large work on the theme *joie de vivre*. The resulting canvases were hung from the factory ceiling over the cigarette-making machines in Zevenaar.

In London the Peter Stuyvesant Foundation was into the performing arts as sponsors. In South Africa the Rembrandt Tobacco Company had no less than three museums and galleries in Graff Reinet, Rupert's birthplace, and his energy in promoting the arts and heritage was everywhere to be seen.

After the column on their Canadian corporate programme, I got a call from Wilmat Tennyson, then president and chief operating officer of Rothman's. Could I meet him and have lunch with him at the Badminton and Racquets Club? When I arrived, he handed me, rather deferentially, a box of Monte Cristo cigars, "which cannot be considered payola," he said, "since I did not know you were writing the column until I read it."

He was of the opinion, he said over lunch, that I had a better grasp of what his company was trying to do than his people had themselves. Would I consider becoming a consultant to Rothman's, advising them on present and future plans and serving as their representative on the Rothman's Gallery board in Stratford?

I considered for two mouthfuls. From being unemployed, I now had two contract jobs that, between them, almost replaced the lost income from *Saturday Night*.

There was another major iron in the fire, too. I had often been on the Elwood Glover lunchtime television show, a CBC production done on location at the old (and first) Four Seasons Hotel opposite the CBC on Jarvis Street. One day, indeed, Tony Roldan, a well-known chef, had cooked a meal for me on TV, the fumes from which brought out the hotel's fire department. Greg Clark, a wonderful old newspaperman and columnist, watching the show in his retirement room in the King Edward Hotel, telephoned me later to say he knew how good it had been. "The look on your face was worth a thousand words," he said, "when you bit into that veal chop."

The producer of the show was Beth Slaney, with whom I had often been involved on various public relations jollifications. I had acted as a commentator for a fashion show at the Room for her (and later taken the models down to the O'Keefe Centre for a party with Flanders and Swann, who were then appearing in *At the Drop of a Hat*). I had myself, together with Charles Templeton, John Robarts, and some other worthies, modelled a suit (one model, one suit made for them by each of several members of the Men's Garment Association). And I had done a flower arrangement in competition for the Toronto Garden Club's Flower Show (a February happening to blow the winter blahs away).

She had suggested doing a television talk show with me as host sometime before. Now seemed a good time. I incorporated Edina

Productions Limited. She sold the idea to CHCH-TV in Hamilton, and jointly we planned twenty-six half-hour programmes to be taped at Robert Lawrence Productions, all twenty-six to be done in the month of January 1971, four per day for five days, and five back-to-back on the sixth.

I had never done more than one show at a time: *Telepoll* at CTV; *Insight* and *Fighting Words* at the CBC. I had no idea what a monster of a schedule was being agreed to.

Through the summer and fall of 1970 we contacted people who would come onto the show, keeping it as entertaining and different as possible. For ballet, for example, we had an utterly adorable young student from the National Ballet School, whose deep violet eyes looking into the camera would have mothers swooning from Cape Race to Nanaimo. She appeared with Celia Franca, but both were followed by Dr. Walpole, a podiatrist who looked after the mangled, tortured feet of the National Ballet dancers on tour. His "survival" kit of plasters, moleskin pads, toe splints, and rubbing alcohol was a revelation; his photographs of some of the most talented feet in the country when wounded were shocking.

We also had Lori Lane, a stripper, on the show. In the newly permissive atmosphere of Toronto she was about to open her own strip show on Yonge Street, just south of Dundas. She was a very self-possessed but provocative woman who, in our first office interview, teased another guest in a way that one could only admire for its skill, even though it was disruptive of a short planning session.

After our taping, I attended her opening show (if, as Beth Slaney would say, you will forgive the expression), and together with other invited guests (including her mother) posed with Lori for a photograph, she clad only in a bikini bottom.

Months later my son was livid with me. After a football game, he had gone on to a party that ended up at Lori Lane's.

"Dad, I could have died. There at the top of the stairs is a full-length, life-size picture of you and the principal stripper. I was embarrassed."

Other sixties personalities queued up to be on the show: Ronnie Hawkins; Colonel Sanders, who had buckets of Kentucky Fried Chicken sent in for the whole crew at the end of his taping; Boris Brott; Nathan Cohen (the last television show he ever did); and Arthur Hailey.

The show ran for one season once a week and was repeated the following summer every night for five weeks on CHCH. But syndication did not materialize and the making of good (we hoped) television cheap (which we did) proved to be more demanding and less satisfying than I had thought.

At the same time as all this was happening I undertook to write, again with Rothman's backing, a brief history of the Toronto Symphony to celebrate its fiftieth anniversary in 1973. This was a fascinating project. There was a great archive of material. The start of the orchestra was almost like a fairy tale. Two wind players from the orchestra of Shea's Hippodrome asked Luigi von Kunitz, director of the Toronto Music Academy, if he would put together a classical symphony with his string players and the various vaudeville wind players. They would perform at 5:00 p.m. — between the matinee and evening performances at the theatres.

He said yes; the concerts were dubbed "Twilight Concerts"; admission was twenty-five cents; and a copy of the opening programme of April 23, 1923, was still in the archives.

The project also brought many interviews with players of the day and attendance at rehearsals as well as performances. But the resulting book, in a golden slipcase for the golden anniversary, was, alas, not widely distributed. The Women's Committee was not enlisted to sell it since it was "not a Women's Committee book," one symphony board member said. But at least Rothman's put it into all the major public and university libraries.

At the same time I was preparing another book, for my consulting and by-now weekly *Financial Post* column still left good swatches of private at-home time.

Eve Orpen, whom I had known for several years as the public relations person for Longman's, had recently formed, with another publishing friend, their own company, Lester and Orpen. She had taken me to lunch and extracted a promise that I would "do her a book." We had originally thought that a book about Canada's summer festivals would suit. I attended most of them now for *The Financial Post*, and had been actively involved with the Guelph Festival from its founding, and was on the board of the Stratford Festival.

However, though I had time to write, I did not have time for concentrated research. So I looked at the columns I had written for the *Canadian Churchman* and decided to make a book out of them.

We had for some years now had a small farmhouse in the country northeast of Toronto — leased, as was Garden Island's cottage — but a great place to escape to. Taking a half-formed idea, plus all the tear sheets, Tish and I went off to Fraser House, near Claremont, in February 1974. She was busy with a script in the main room for touring the medieval galleries at the Royal Ontario Museum where she was now a docent. I was at the kitchen table with my stuff.

Starting with the first column I had written for *The Financial Post*, a nostalgic piece about the carol service in King's College, Cambridge, I proceeded to write a day-by-day account of one man's Christian year. Some of the longer pieces were from the *Churchman*; one or two were from *The Financial Post*. With the Prayer Book list of saints' days in front of me, the days of winter silence lengthening into two weeks' holiday, I wrote a whole lot of intervening shorter pieces from a general church file I had kept for ideas for years.

At the end of March I delivered a manuscript to Eve Orpen,

saying it was not what she had asked for, but what I had wanted
to do. Within a week Malcolm Lester got in touch with me. "We
love it, Arnold. We want to do it. But tell me," he said over the
telephone, "what in hell is Epifanny?" (Epiphany was not one of
the Jewish feasts that both he and Eve knew.)

I was both amused and touched. A new publishing firm, owned
and run by two members of the Jewish faith, was going to publish
a book that was, as the foreword said, "a sort of Christian diary."

The title, *Some Camel, Some Needle*, referred to one piece in the
book which, in quoting the New Testament injunction that it would
be easier for a camel to go through the eye of a needle than for a
rich man to enter heaven, had said of rich churches, "some camel,
some needle," a deliberate parody of Winston Churchill's great
remark during the war about England, "some chicken, some neck."

Writing day after day in the winter countryside with Tish
equally bookish in the next room was a memorable experience,
more memorable even than the launch of the book together with
two other Lester and Orpen authors: Morley Torgov (*The Life of
Maximilian Glick*) and Doug Hall, who wrote novels and ran (still
runs) an interview show on CHCH-TV in Hamilton.

The books and the columns, the speeches and the television,
easily replaced *Saturday Night*'s income. They could not, alas,
cover *Saturday Night*'s debts.

With two of our three children now gone from the family home,
and the third only one year away from university, we did the only
thing possible: we sold our house. We had paid $41,500 for it in
1964 and had invested another $15,000 in it. We thought our-
selves very clever to sell it for $115,000 in 1973. A large Rosedale
house, it would now list for a minimum of one million dollars.

So, by 1974, we were installed in a comfortable rented town
house, our *Saturday Night* debts paid. With the tiny remnant of
capital left from all that I had ever accumulated in Canada, we all
planned to take off for our son's wedding in London, England.

Beyond that we could not clearly see. I felt that Edina Productions was thriving. I had had major writing contracts from the Ontario Hospital Association, the Royal Commission on Ontario Hydro, and the Ontario government's Department of Tourism. Maybe I should expand, get a larger office (I had already outgrown my house-office, much to Tish's relief), and get some associates.

I was leery of this, though. My writing skills were adequate for what I was doing. The consulting seemed to be effective. But as an entrepreneur and businessman, my heart at *Saturday Night* had ruled my head to my total financial disaster. My business skills were, it seemed to me, minimal.

At which point another *Financial Post* column saved me.

XVIII

THE CULTURAL
EXPLOSION

B Y THE MID-SEVENTIES A TRUE cultural explosion had happened in Canada. Basically due to the centennial in 1967, new
arts facilities had been built in Charlottetown (the first), Toronto,
Winnipeg, Edmonton, Saskatoon, and Victoria. A viable regional
theatre was in operation with companies in Victoria, Vancouver,
Calgary, Edmonton, Regina, Winnipeg, Halifax, Quebec City,
Fredericton, Hamilton, and London. The National Arts Centre
had opened in 1969. The Art Gallery of Toronto had become the
Art Gallery of Ontario and tripled in size.

Our family was up to their necks in it. Kip (Christine), the
eldest, had been a member of the touring company of *You're a Good
Man, Charlie Brown* for three years in Toronto, Montreal, Buffalo
and, for over eighteen months, Chicago. Alastair had, together
with another boy, founded a poetry festival at Upper Canada
College, as well as being defensive cocaptain of the league-win-
ning football team. Sarah had won the Churchill Gold Medal for
public speaking (reckoned an art in our house, she said) in open
competition with all the local boys independent schools. Tish had
become a tour guide (later called "docent") at the Royal Ontario
Museum and did yeoman service guiding the public around the
extraordinary Chinese exhibition, "The Archaeological Finds of
the People's Republic of China."

I had now been arts consultant to Rothman's for four years. In that time, with their sponsorship, I had written a short celebratory history of the Toronto Symphony and a similar one for the Edmonton Symphony. I had been sent on a tour of their companies in Britain, Holland, and South Africa. Together with Richard Graburn, the director of Rothman's Gallery in Stratford, I had spent a fair amount of money acquiring a collection of prints for their Canadian offices. We had also chosen three major outdoor sculptures for the Stratford gallery grounds. Two of these were by Ontario sculptors who lived near London. Ed Zelenak was into large, semitransparent tube sculptures, and one of his works seemed appropriate for the pond at the gallery. Walter Redinger worked in large plastic. Up in the woods, just by the parking lot, his *Caucasian Totems* fitted beautifully.

A major work called *Athabasca*, by Robert Murray, a Canadian by then domiciled in Connecticut, was installed between the gallery entrance and the entrance to the parking lot. A strong piece, it was unfortunately sited so as to look more like an antiaircraft gun emplacement than the work of art it undoubtedly is.

For Rothman's Graburn and I had visited galleries and studios all over Canada. Wilmat Tennyson was pleased with our efforts. So was John Devlin, the chairman.

I had had a crash course in the visual arts.

The columns in *The Financial Post*, written from almost every major city in Canada, had also been a learning experience. I had always believed that Toronto was not the cultural capital it claimed to be. Attendance at the Manitoba Opera, the Calgary Philharmonic, Les Grands Ballets Canadiens, the Vancouver Symphony, Neptune Theatre in Halifax, and Theatre London had shown the rich variety and quality of the performing arts post-Expo — the watershed year when support by government was no longer confined to the interest on the Canada Council's endowment fund, but was now a transfer from tax revenues. (Without such a basic shift in principle, most large arts groups and a host of smaller ones would have collapsed from their efforts to showcase themselves at Mayor Jean Drapeau's incredible Expo 67.)

In the affluent seventies the arts were certainly booming. So were their bills. It was clear that the federal government, having started something, needed other partners in this exciting but expensive business. André Fortier, a man dedicated to promoting and nurturing the artistic life of Canada, asked Ed Bovey, then chief executive officer of a natural gas company in Toronto, to lead a committee to investigate how business — the private sector — could become more involved.

Bovey had been in the thick of the arts scene ever since he had been one of a small group of businessmen who had finally secured Henry Moore's *The Archer* for the new Nathan Phillips Square in Toronto. He had, together with Fred Eaton, raised the money to expand the Art Gallery of Toronto into the Art Gallery of Ontario. He was active on the board of the Toronto Symphony and of Massey Hall.

Fortier was the under-secretary of state through whom all Canada Council budgets flowed. His proposition was simple: "let's find out where the arts are heading, what it's going to cost, and where the money is to come from, because the government cannot, and should not, find it all."

Bovey said yes. (Bovey nearly always said yes to a challenge). He also, together with Fortier, persuaded a blue-chip group of businessmen to say yes, too: John Prentice, head of Canadian Forest Products in British Columbia; Donald Harvie, senior vice president of Petrofina Canada Limited in Calgary; Jim Burns, president of Great-West Life Assurance Company of Winnipeg; Paul Desmarais of Power Corporation in Montreal; Jean Ostiguy, senior partner of Crang & Ostiguy, also from Montreal; and Trevor Housser, the head of Imperial Oil in the Maritimes.

They had commissioned a study in 1972, which was now ready

to be published. It showed, on a continuous line graph, that if the arts were to continue expanding, business and private support would have to shoulder a good deal more of that expansion expense than they currently did.

I wrote a column in the *Post*, supporting the work of the committee:

> *The idea of working with the business community to support the cultural quality of life is a very healthy one. Both business and the creative artist or performer can learn lessons from each other.*

> *Example?*

> *Any industrial company should be so lucky as to have the corporate loyalty that is commonplace in a theatrical or ballet company. Or the same sense of decision-making truly shared by board and employees. Or even the voluntary sacrifice of immediate income for the long-run good of the organization.*

I also pointed out that it would be unwise to take the Business Committee for the Arts in the United States as an exact model:

> *There are differences here in Canada in business as well as in the tax-supported funding agencies. There is not, for example, the same spread of major companies across the country as there is in the United States. Corporate decisions are taken in far fewer centres. There is also the question of the head offices of some subsidiary companies [here] not being head offices at all.*

There was a well-articulated, tax-subsidized national funding for the arts in Canada, but not in the United States. Nor did the United States have such hugely subsidized "consumers" of artistic product as the state-owned CBC and National Film Board.

As Wilmat Tennyson had before, so Bovey did now. Having read the column, he asked if I would drop in to talk about it. Walking by all the well-chosen collection of Canadian contemporary art on his headquarter walls at Northern and Central Gas Company, I was convinced that he knew what he wanted to do — get more businesses to follow his lead.

He told me that the committee had invited the chief executive officers of the top one hundred companies in Canada, plus some others who, though not top in sales or assets, were known for their support of cultural organizations, to a meeting in Ottawa.

"André Fortier," Bovey continued, "has also arranged for the governor-general to invite them to dinner afterwards with their spouses. The invitations to the meeting have gone to their business addresses, and the invitations to Government House have gone to their home addresses. André reckons that will give us a few more at the meeting than we might otherwise get." Then he asked me if I could attend the meeting as a consultant.

I said that I would really like to be there, but that I had a speaking engagement in London, Ontario, that night. "It is also about business and the arts. It's the banquet speech to the annual meeting of the University of Western Ontario's School of Business Alumni."

"Well, you couldn't make the dinner, but you could come in the afternoon and then fly to London from Ottawa."

"There isn't a plane."

"Yes, there is. There's my company plane. If you get to Ottawa, I'll get you to London and home."

This was generosity: company planes are expensive. This was also determination: Ed wanted me there. I thought he wanted *The Financial Post* to be there so we could do a follow-up. In any case, I agreed, thanked him, said that I would be pleased to help in any way, and left.

The joint strategy of Fortier and Bovey worked. There were

over sixty top executives, consultants, and steering committee members who arrived at the high-ceilinged reception room at the National Arts Centre on the afternoon of June 6.

The people who had done the report on arts funding gave a detailed, persuasive account of where the arts were going, what it was costing, what the benefits were, and concluded that if business and the private sector were to come up with fifteen percent of the total budget, box office, gallery entrance fees, and earned revenue from special events would provide another fifty percent, leaving thirty-five percent of the total for government support at all three levels — municipal, provincial, and federal.

After the presentation, a coffee break was called. Jean Ostiguy, Ed's Quebec lieutenant on the original committee, and Ed walked over to me and asked me to walk into the corridor with them.

"I think we've got their ear," Ed said, "and we should in the next session ask for their support in setting up an organization like the Business Committee for the Arts. Not the same, as you have pointed out, but to achieve the same ends in our context. If we can get it going, will you run it for us?"

Without hesitation I said yes, and we went back into the meeting room where, after some discussion, agreement was reached to set up such a body.

I flew off to London at 4:30 and had time to think of what was ahead. I knew the major arts groups across the country. I had written about most of them in *The Financial Post*. I knew Bovey. I thought people like John Devlin of Rothman's, George Sinclair, head of MacLaren Advertising, and Fred Eaton would join those members of the steering committee who chose to stay as board members of the new organization.

My company could still function if I retained my writing contract with the *Post*, and it would be in all our interests, business, arts, and the *Post* if I did so.

There seemed in my present role and the planned one a certain synergy, as people later would call it, and certainly, for both groups, economy of scale.

About business, and my entrée into it at the top level, I was less sure, though I had two things going for me. I had run a business and met a payroll for almost ten years at *Saturday Night*, and I had kept things afloat and prospered as the president of Edina Productions Limited. Furthermore, while pursuing advertising contracts for *Saturday Night*, I had met a fair number of the people who had attended the meeting.

Everything looked feasible as we touched down in London and I went off to talk to another lot of businessmen: men, I realized, who could now be important contacts rather than just a congenial audience.

And so, back late at night to Tish. She was as excited as I was at the prospect. "But Alastair is being married next month in England," she said. "You can't start until August."

Which is what I reported to Bovey the next day.

"Suits us," he said. "Now I don't want you to be executive director of this thing. That implies you would implement what we propose. The reason we want you is for you to develop policy and report to us what you want to do, how you want to do it, and what it will cost. We are talking about president and chief executive officer of the organization."

Naive as I was about business structures and protocol, I agreed without realizing what a huge difference this would make in my relations with business. CEO talks to CEO. CEOs get invited to conference board meetings. CEOs have authority to do things and tell their board why afterwards, not ask for permission first.

So the title and position were settled. I mentioned that I would like to keep up my writing for the *Post* and the *Canadian Churchman*. And there would be other commitments (I was also chairman of an RESP organization, the International Scholarship Foundation).

"Let us agree, then, that you take one day a week for your own company," Bovey said, "and the other four for us."

Again an eminently sensible solution.

A salary, conditions of employment, and a budget for the next five months was agreed upon. We shook hands and I said how much I looked forward to the next five years, which was all I promised. Then I flew off to England the next day to attend my son's wedding in London, after which Sarah went on the obligatory European tour most seventeen-year-olds were now taking and we went to the Outer Hebrides to discover grandfather's grave.

Renewed, eager, and excited, I arrived back in Toronto to start the Council for Business and the Arts in Canada on August 1, 1974.

XIX

CANADIAN MEDICIS

B USINESS HAS ALWAYS BEEN INVOLVED in the arts in Western civilization. The Medicis were bankers before they were connoisseurs, and the monks who built great medieval abbeys were essentially large business corporations using Mammon to serve God.

Even in such a recent and fragile civilization as Canada's, businessmen had both practised art as amateurs and been patrons of the few professional artists. Cornelius Van Horne painted oils of the CPR landscape as he pushed the rails through to the West Coast. But he also commissioned artists to do better pictures for his parlour cars and his advertising.

In more recent times Canada Packers, under J. S. Maclean, had put together a first-rate collection of contemporary art by the Group of Seven when the actual seven were poor and struggling. Canada Packers also sponsored the Toronto Symphony Orchestra's Sunday afternoon concerts in Massey Hall.

By the time of the Ottawa conference in 1974, Ed Bovey had put together a remarkable art collection for the corporate offices of Northern and Central Gas. Texaco was up to its eyes in opera, both in Canada and the United States. Bob McMichael and his wife had amassed a Group of Seven collection so large they had to build a gallery to put it in.

I had worked for Rothman's for four years and knew how they used both the performing and visual arts for their own purposes, even while seeming to the outside world to be merely generous patrons.

I also knew the timidity and total lack of any underlying philosophy in most corporate boardrooms when the arts were discussed. It was, after all, shareholders' money that was being spent, and it was less than fifty years since an aggrieved shareholder of a Toronto bank had sued the directors for giving $25,000 to the Toronto General Hospital's building campaign. He lost the case, but the memory of the fight was deeply entrenched. So, while giving to hospitals, the United Community Fund, universities, and community groups was now accepted, the arts were a frill to most businessmen. Money given to them was suspect and could be challenged.

Stereotypes were not all on the business side. Art gallery directors could be very leery of corporate involvement. When Rothman's presented Stratford with an art gallery as a centennial project, then put up $100,000 a year to run it, some Sunday painters in Stratford were affronted. The change of the name to Rothman's Gallery Stratford irked them; the large and superb exhibitions from abroad irked them; the loss of their control to professional curators irked them.

It came to a head when a local amateur wrote to the *Stratford Beacon Herald* and asked why Rothman's was always so preeminent in the affairs of the gallery. "What have they ever done for us except give money?" she wanted to know.

Wilmat Tennyson's reply was swift and final. "Let us not hurt her feelings anymore," he said. "Cancel the money."

It was not just Stratford. When Rothman's wanted to have a banner over the main door of the Royal Ontario Museum saying "Rothman's presents" the exhibition of Australian aboriginal art inside, the request was turned down flatly. The Art Gallery of Ontario would never (and did never) take a Rothman's touring exhibition. Nor did the National Gallery.

No wonder that the total amount given to the arts by business was less than two million dollars when the new council opened its offices in September 1974.

I had had one meeting with the steering committee and several with Ed Bovey before that happened. Bovey made one thing clear, and his steering committee emphasized it: I was the chief executive officer and my contract said "the control and management of the business of the council are hereby committed to the president."

"An executive director," Bovey said, "implements what his or her board decides. As president and chief executive officer, you will decide what to do and report to the board why, how, and what cost, just as a CEO does in a commercial business."

Just what to do was fairly clear in my mind. Two years before, as a result of my dealing with business people through *The Financial Post* column, I had sought a meeting with Louis Applebaum, then executive director of the Ontario Arts Council, and Arthur Gelber, patron-at-large, institutor of many good arts-oriented initiatives with government (though not with business), and a member of Applebaum's board.

In a memo that minuted this meeting I had written:

It was agreed that what was now needed was

(i) *a clear definition of aims and objectives for new business participation in the arts;*

(ii) *a clear statement of the benefits that could accrue both in the public relations area for business and in the quality of life in society generally;*

(iii) *a plan of action that might start with*

(a) *small meetings between the various parties herein named;*

(b) *an agreement on a plan that would bring in the two councils (Canada and Ontario);*

(c) *perhaps* The Financial Post *on one of its FP-CBC reports.*

Before we could follow up we heard that the Canada Council had taken the matter out of our hands. With the report high-lighted at the Ottawa meeting and the result of its recommendations, it was now squarely back in mine.

The first thing the new body had to do was to make it clear that we were not a fund-raising entity. We merely wanted to persuade business to put more money from their discretionary funding into the arts. We would counsel them as to how that could be done with significant benefit to them. We would also undertake to talk to arts groups and suggest ways in which they might more easily avail themselves of business expertise in the better getting and spending of their private funding.

Honest brokers, we thought we might be.

Ed Bovey called a press conference to explain what we had in mind. I spoke as to method. Regretting the lack of any solid statistics about the arts sector, I said that the gathering of such information would be a priority. The Canada Council's figures from arts organizations were confidential. The Statistics Canada figures were too wide-ranging, and too out of date. Assembled one year, processed the next, they came out as annualized general figures. Looking at them, one was reminded of Robert Stanfield's great remark in the House of Commons about annualized unemployment figures: "The annualized temperature in Ottawa at this moment is probably forty degrees Fahrenheit. But I warn you, go outside and you'll freeze your buns off."

So we had two functions. First, to be a service centre for the arts and business, offering valid statistics and information about both groups one to the other. The second, as Bovey never tired of saying to me, was to be missionaries. We had to persuade business to become involved; we had to persuade the arts to let them.

Business welcomed the foundation of the council. Bovey and his steering committee had seen to that. The arts groups were less sure. If we were not going to raise money and distribute it, what *were* we going to do?

We had said we would finance our operations by asking businesses to become members at $1,000 per year. Some businesses wanted to know what exactly they would get in return for their money. One chief executive officer, a board member of the National Ballet, said he was appalled at the thought of us taking $50,000 out of the arts pot if fifty companies joined. Some arts groups shared his opinion. Were we not taking out rather than raising the amount to be put in? It was going to be a long road ahead. I could see that.

Nevertheless, with an initial grant of $25,000 from the Canada Council (to be repaid someday if we got rolling), we set up offices in the Toronto Dominion Centre. The staff was merely myself and my secretary, Merle Kerr, transferred from my old Edina Productions office.

The first job was to get letters patent, to become incorporated, and to transform the steering committee, with some additions, into a board of directors.

The mission statement was agreed to, and the name Canadian Council for Business and the Arts was applied for. Weeks went by. Constant nit-picking from Ottawa's Department of Consumer and Corporate Affairs held us up, despite the fact that Osler

Hoskin, Northern and Central's lawyers, who were, at Northern and Central's expense, acting for us, were well-known and might have expected a speedy reply.

Then I found out the reason. Ken Dryden, goalie for the Montreal Canadiens, was the articling student handling matters for the Osler Hoskin partner, Jim Kennedy. The contact in Ottawa was a francophone woman who liked to talk to her hockey idol. André Fortier intervened, and we got our incorporation.

Now we had to finance ourselves. Using the list of attendees at the June conference in Ottawa, plus others whom board members had suggested at our first board meeting on November 6, we sent out invitations to join the new council between Christmas and New Year.

Different board members signed the letter. For me it was a quick insight into corporate power. Page Wadsworth, head of the Canadian Imperial Bank of Commerce, sent out fourteen letters; thirteen joined. Bovey sent some fifty, in essence all those not picked up by other board members, as well as his own list. At least thirty joined. He had said that if we got forty members in the first two months, we were in business. By the beginning of March we had fifty-five. We were in business.

It was a business I was delighted to be in. I loved the arts. Over the previous fifteen years I had seen a great deal of what this country could achieve. As editor of *Saturday Night*, I knew the writing fraternity well. As a theatre critic, I had seen most of the regional theatre. Since I had started to write for *The Financial Post*, I had widened my geographical range; since my involvement with Rothman's, I had given myself a crash course in the visual arts. As a newly elected board member of Massey Hall, I was listening to a lot of music. The impetus given by the centennial, by Expo 67, and by such federal programmes as Opportunities for Youth and Local Initiatives Programme had transformed the quality, variety, and availability of the arts in Canada. The new arts facilities in Ottawa, Winnipeg, Victoria, Charlottetown, Montreal, and Toronto had raised both the level of production standards and the comfort index of the audience.

When Tish and I arrived in Canada in 1947, there were a mere half-dozen professional symphony orchestras, no professional theatre, no theatre buildings even, and only a couple of purpose-built music halls still operating. Now there was a network of regional theatre, likewise of art galleries and professional dance and ballet companies in four metropolitan centres: Vancouver, Winnipeg, Toronto, and Montreal.

Expectations had been raised. Money had to be found to fulfill them. In our uniquely mixed economy where communications had always been a federal matter and consequently a federal expense, we had to involve the market economy more in these burgeoning creative endeavours.

To be at the very centre of it was overwhelming, both in its demands and its rewards. Between the first board meeting in November 1974 and the second one in May 1975, I had visited Regina, Stratford, Victoria, Vancouver, Edmonton, Calgary, Kingston, Ottawa, Montreal, Winnipeg, Niagara-on-the-Lake, Hamilton, Moose Jaw, Prince Albert, Banff, and Guelph.

In *The Financial Post* I had written columns about the opening of the new Art Gallery of Ontario and about a meeting in Ottawa with a group of "arts" senators from Washington, D.C. I had reviewed shows by Regina's Globe Theatre, Toronto Workshop Productions, the National Ballet at the O'Keefe Centre, Theatre London, the Edmonton Opera Association, the Citadel Theatre in Edmonton, the Stratford Festival on tour at Montreal's Place des Arts, and the Manitoba Opera.

But there was more now than just going to the shows at all these places. I met with the boards of directors of the various theatres, usually at lunch or dinner before the show, to discuss their aims and financial objectives. Even in good times expansion was making heavy demands on funds. Provincial councils were being formed. I had been invited by Horst Schmidt, minister in charge of Alberta Culture, to see how the Alberta government could best design its support of the arts. I had met with the director of British Columbia's funding agency. Ed Bovey and I sought regular meetings with the chairman and senior directors of the Ontario Arts Council.

I went to New York to discuss the methods and programmes of the Business Committee for the Arts. I was part of the faculty at two conferences about the responsibility of arts organization board members at the Banff Centre. I attended the Canadian Conference of the Arts annual conference and met with half a dozen or more arts groups per week, either in the offices in Toronto or my hotel room in various cities across the country.

I also went back to the corporate boardrooms and executive offices of the major corporations where I had tried to sell them advertising in *Saturday Night*. Now I wanted merely to sell them an idea.

The weekly column in the *Post* kept my name in front of business people. The directors of the council in each city arranged meetings with people I did not know.

There was a stir in the air. No doubt about that. Business was not averse to getting involved, providing they had some kind of guidelines, some kind of assurance that what they were looking at made sense to people who knew more about it than they did. Time and time again a business person would say: "We know how to make aluminum (or cars, or wood pulp), but we know nothing about making music or theatre. Show us how and we'll give it a shot."

Copies of a speech I had given at the Empire Club, "The High Cost of Leisure," were sent out daily. Ed Bovey, John Devlin, and John Prentice also took to the public platform. People like Smiley

Raborn in Calgary and Trevor Housser in Halifax got groups of people together to listen to the message. Boards of some major (and many minor) arts organizations asked a rep from the CBAC to talk to them (it was often me).

As this began to jell, we needed the facts and figures I had spoken of at the initial press conference.

Al Kowalenko, a recent Ryerson Institute graduate in journalism, came on staff charged with the task of developing and administering a set of statistical surveys. The aim was to discover what the actual flow of funds was for any arts organization in the country with a budget over $100,000. In two parts the survey showed actuals for the current reporting year and budget predictions for the coming year. The purpose was to show the corporate donations committees of our members what was expected from the private sector, and how that jibed with government subventions and revenue earned from box office in the performing arts and entrance fees from museums and galleries in the visual.

Getting the figures was difficult. Not many arts groups had had that kind of public scrutiny. But Kowalenko was a determined, single-minded man. He worked on his own at a desk in Northern and Central's offices; there was no room for him in our own office. He was methodical, ritualistically punctual at arriving and leaving, dogged with backsliders, endlessly patient with figures that didn't add up, couldn't be reconciled, or were wrongly distributed within the various category columns. All this thirty floors above us in the same building.

Al was no barrel of laughs in the office (when he was there), but the CBAC surveys are his permanent monument, though much refined, enlarged, and sophisticated since his day.

What they did was not just tell our corporate members where the arts groups were, but told the arts groups about one another.

Roger Selby, then director of the Winnipeg Art Gallery, took the municipal and provincial figures from the survey in other areas and went, in honest rage, to the equivalent authorities in Manitoba to *prove* to them, as he said, what a bunch of penny-pinching cheapskates they were.

Glenn Cumming, when I went over to Hamilton one day to see the new gallery's collection of Karel Appel's work, asked me when the next survey would be out.

"In about a month," I said. "Why?"

"Oh," he said. "When that comes it's like Christmas. I pore over it and compare things to buttress every argument I can make to my board and through them to funders and corporate patrons. I lock my door and go at it for a whole day. It's the most intellectually stimulating thing that comes into the office — and it is unrivalled in its unvarnished statements about the competition."

Within five years we had travelled a fair way along the road I had foreseen. The surveys were not only accepted by business who paid for them and the arts groups who provided their figures, but by government. It gave us great glee in the office during the elections of 1980-81 to hear John Roberts and David Macdonald quoting *our* figures in their electioneering.

"That's what it's all about," Bovey said. "A business group with a staff of three giving better figures than a government department of three hundred."

Our staff of three consisted of myself, Sarah Iley, my daughter, who had come in when Al Kowalenko had gone off to do public relations proper at Tisdall Clark, and Eileen Love, who had replaced Merle Kerr when she left to start a family. From an essentially joe-job status Sarah lifted research and communications into a powerful part of the office. Eileen, whose skills in typing and shorthand were phenomenal, was equally not just a secretary. She took over the books, sent out the invoices, dealt with the whole management of the office, and faithfully reproduced speeches, articles, and reports sent to her from all over the world.

We were a family. Dedicated. Hugely enjoying what we were doing. All of us growing in the job as the job itself grew.

We produced four to six newsletters a year and three sets of surveys; ran two competitions; produced four booklets — on boards, sponsorship, corporate funding, and corporate art — which have sold more than forty thousand copies, all written by Sarah and handled by Eileen.

At the end of my tenure as president, fifteen years and three chairmen later, that small office group, with another added just three years ago, were still there and the initial objective we had set ourselves had been reached. We had helped to increase the amount of private money put at the service of the arts at least tenfold. We had helped to bring in the whole concept of sponsorship, which is now itself big business. We had created *The Financial Post* Awards for Business in the Arts and operated it for ten years. We had created and awarded the CBAC Award for five years.

We had made business support of the arts viable, worthwhile both for business and the arts, and watched the arts themselves grow exceptionally in that time.

XX

TRAVELLING ARTS SALESMAN

WITHIN A YEAR OR TWO WE HAD over a hundred members of the Council for Business and the Arts. Our expenses and revenues were pretty evenly matched. The three of us that were the whole staff were no longer inventing our role: we were actually fulfilling it.

My job was the mission. So I was more out of the office than in it. And what I saw in my travels was the rapid creation of a truly Canadian cultural network.

Take the plays, for a start. For years summer stock and the fledgling regional network had relied on a mix of Broadway and West End plays old enough to have Canadian rights available (i.e., they were no longer protected, having run their economic course in those two centres) plus the odd classical play or thirties farce. No longer. The Globe Theatre in Regina now had a permanent playwright-in-residence. Vancouver's Arts Club Theatre ran a Noël Coward play, *Hay Fever*, at its original theatre in downtown Vancouver, making enough profit to build two new spaces on Granville Island where they produced mainly Canadian plays.

In Saskatoon Twenty-fifth Street House Theatre produced a cooperatively written play, *Paper Wheat*, sponsored by the Federated Co-ops of that province. Its theme and content was the struggle between the producer and the middleman, the farmer and the elevator company. The characters were prairie characters. There was an unhandy but disciplined English couple desperately trying to learn farming as a step to a richer and fuller life than overcrowded industrial England could provide (shades of my Uncle Harry). There was a Ukrainian family, all hard work and some agricultural knowledge. And there was a Canadian, born in Canada, working for the elevator.

The direction of the play was superb. No one who saw the English couple tell of their fight with the weather by folding and unfolding a blanket on a table will ever forget it. On tour it went to the NAC in Ottawa. In the studio theatre there an audience of mainly civil servants got so involved that when a vote was called for to set up a co-op to market their grain, all the present-day civil servants became, for a moment, farmers of 1910 and voted for it en bloc.

What Twenty-fifth Street Theatre did in Saskatoon, Toronto Workshop Productions had done in Toronto. A similarly collective creation, *Hey Rube*, a dazzling play about a circus in a small town, was remounted several times. And Theatre Passe Muraille had even more success with *The Farm Show*, based on what members of the company had learned from living for several weeks in the farming community of Clinton in Southwestern Ontario.

Paper Wheat and *The Farm Show* were the products of a new generation of theatre, and they paved the way for what became known as alternative theatre — alternative in its funding, content, and audience.

Out of those 1970 initiatives (*The Farm Show* was produced originally in 1972, toured Canada, and went to Britain from 1974-79; *Paper Wheat* was produced in 1977 and toured through 1979) came the creation of other plays based on the Canadian experience, leading to the founding, indirectly, of the Blyth Festival, the Huron County Playhouse, and other community-centred theatres.

Individual playwrights also proved that Canadian plays could command an audience, and that they could tour from one region to another. I saw *Waiting for the Parade*, a powerful play about women in wartime, at the Stephenville Festival in Newfoundland, but it had been written seven years before in Calgary by John Murrell. *Billy Bishop Goes to War*, written by Vancouver playwright John Gray, premiered in 1978 at the Vancouver East Cultural Centre. I saw it five years later at the Academy Theatre in Lindsay, Ontario.

The amount, the standards, the themes of theatrical activity now were all light-years away from the Dominion Drama Festival, yet *Overlaid*, in which I was so suddenly involved in Ottawa while a member of the Queen's Faculty Players, had been so comparatively recent as 1949. For *The Financial Post*, and as a messenger and potential helper from CBAC, I visited theatres in Stephenville, Newfoundland; Kelowna, British Columbia; Blyth, Ontario; Lennoxville, Quebec; Chatham, New Brunswick; Lindsay, Ontario; Mulgrave Road, Nova Scotia; and Yellowknife in the Northwest Territories.

Not only were there companies performing in these places, there were facilities — proper, purpose-built, or converted facilities — in which they could perform.

Part of this conversion was due to old opera houses that had been closed by movie distributors in the 1920s to abolish competition coming back onto the market. That was how Lindsay, through the persistence of Dennis Sweeting, got the Academy Theatre back (with Johnny Wayne helping a benefit for it), and that was how Kingston got its Grand Theatre back for the Kingston Symphony as well as for local theatre groups.

It seemed almost every year that a great new place for entertainment was being opened. In April 1977 the old Orpheum Theatre was reopened, refurbished, and acoustically treated to become the home of the Vancouver Symphony. In 1980 the

Centre-in-the-Square, a beautiful auditorium on one side and an art gallery on the other, opened in Kitchener, Ontario. In 1981 the old city hall in Regina was reopened as the home of Ken Kramer's Globe Theatre.

In 1982, what had been called for several years while it was under consideration and construction, the New Massey Hall, was opened as the Roy Thomson Hall, home of the Toronto Symphony and the Toronto Mendelssohn Choir. In 1983 the Grand Theatre in London was reclaimed from the movie industry and reopened, as indeed a grand theatre for Theatre London. And in 1984 the Northern Arts and Cultural Centre was opened in Yellowknife, Northwest Territories.

That was an opening to end all openings. For a start, Yellowknife is not exactly a metropolitan centre. Nor was it, up to that time, considered a possible venue for touring companies. But local pressure, the availability of a no-longer-needed space in the huge central high school, and the dogged support of the *Globe and Mail* brought into being a superb 450-seat facility.

The party began at 6:30 for eight, with champagne. The first half of the show lasted until 9:30. Intermission continued until ten. The stunning second-half show featured Diane Dupuy's Famous People Players and Bonnie Baker, Canada's version of Dolly Parton, introduced by Peter Gzowski. Then, still in twilight at 11:15, we went off to the real party, which I left as the sun came up at 2:30 a.m.

Light-years from the Dominion Drama Festival in Ottawa?

Outer space, that was.

The pace kept up with the Calgary Performing Arts Centre in October of that year, whose opening lasted for a whole week with a symphony concert, two plays, and a variety show.

Nor were the visual arts left behind. Kitchener had a new art gallery in the Centre-in-the-Square. The London Regional Art Gallery, a vast new space, looking for all the world like two silos lying horizontally on the ground, opened in 1980. The Jesuits gave their collection to the people of Quebec City and housed them in a converted convent that opened as La Nouvelle Musée de la Séminaire in 1982.

The next year Vancouver took its tiny art gallery to court and reopened in the monumental spaces of the old courthouse, right in the middle of Vancouver. The Beaverbrook Museum in Fredericton added two new wings in 1983, almost doubling its exhibition space. Finally, for the visual art community, everything was topped off by the opening of the new National Gallery in 1988 and the Museum of Civilization in 1989.

All but these last two (and the Northern Arts and Cultural Centre) had been built with funds raised on a fairly regular formula: one-third federal, one-third provincial and municipal, and one-third private.

That meant that a lot of board members — certainly the business people board members — had spent a lot of time raising money. And not just for the facilities. New and expanded spaces demand expanded funds to operate them.

It was our job at CBAC to work with boards people, specifically and in general, to see just what the implications were and what sources of capital and operating funds would be necessary.

We joined forces with the Banff Centre in this venture and ran three-day seminars at Banff for the West, at the Niagara Institute for the centre, and in Halifax for the Maritimes.

We talked of the legal responsibilities of board members — or at least Aaron Milrad did. We talked of taxation breaks for gifts. We talked of board organization, the sources for good board members, and especially of communication between the board members themselves, the board and the staff (especially the artistic director), and the board and the community.

Banff and Niagara-on-the-Lake are both, in their own ways, spectacular settings. Banff has the mountains; the Niagara Institute has its fragrant garden. There was a continuous pressure on the speaker, or discussion leader, to keep his seminar members' minds on the subject. There was always the awful moment when you saw the daydream in the skiers' or gardeners' eyes in front of you. But by discussing such matters, by providing them with the CBAC's three booklets on boards, sponsorship, and fund-raising, we felt ourselves an integral part of what was no less than a cultural explosion over these years.

I could speak from experience about boards. I had served on the Stratford Festival board throughout Robin Phillips's golden years there. I had been (and still am) involved with Massey Hall and its new sister, Roy Thomson Hall. From Arthur Erickson's first bringing in to a board meeting his wedding-cake-size conceptual model to the glorious opening weeks some six years later, the experience of working for it, watching it grow, involving the public in it, and raising the money for it was exhilarating. But no more so than serving on the board of the Elliot Lake Centre, a community facility in a Northern Ontario mining town which, in the twenty years I was involved, went from bust to boom to bust again. The resilience of the Elliot Lake people, the shrewdness of Dr. Franc Joubin, whose advice kept the centre in funds when the rest of the town could not, the feeling of creating something useful and imaginative in a harsh climate and landscape, made endless waits in small airports while getting in and out worthwhile. It also helped when delegates from smaller centres to our board conferences complained that the faculty knew nothing of their particular problems. You cannot get much smaller in the arts than the Elliot Lake Centre.

Two major schemes got great support and made notable contributions to making boards better. The first was the Young in Art programme. This was first devised by a director of the CBAC, Lyman Henderson.

Why not, he suggested, get a group of chief executive officers together and ask them to give access to their middle-management people as potential arts boards members? He would persuade the CEOs, being one himself, as well as the owner of his company, Davis and Henderson, that such board service would be the best training for executive positions that could be devised.

"They will have to take decisions, which in the corporate bureaucracy they are not yet allowed to take. They will have responsibility for executing those decisions, even raising the money to do so. And if they fail, they will have to explain to the public and their organization why."

Within five years the plan had been implemented in Vancouver, Edmonton, Calgary, Winnipeg, Toronto, Montreal, and Halifax, with well over one hundred arts groups receiving handpicked new members to their boards.

The energy of these volunteers, plus their special expertise, made their way up the arts board ladder a good deal swifter than their corporate one: three of the first batch of middle managers became presidents of their arts group within two years.

The second scheme was in conjunction with *The Financial Post*, which was now firmly allied with us in *The Financial Post* Awards for Business in the Arts. Why not, I suggested to *The Financial Post* conferences manager, have a conference on sponsorship?

Business sponsorship of the arts has grown enormously. Corporations divert money from marketing and corporate relations budgets with specific marketing and corporate image returns in mind.

Well established in sport, and well established in the arts in the United States, there was no real concept of it in Canadian business in the early 1980s. We felt that the arts did not know how to ask, and business did not know how to respond.

Reluctantly the conference manager, Ken Scott, with some pressure from his divisional head at Maclean Hunter, Jim Warrillow, set aside time for such a conference with CBAC programming it.

Sponsorship is now a three-billion-dollar business worldwide in sports and arts. Not only does *The Financial Post* hold conferences on it regularly, so does *The Sponsorship Report*, owned, ironically but enthusiastically by the same Ken Scott.

These conferences, at first attended by arts groups and sports associations looking for money, are now more heavily attended by business people looking for ways to spend money effectively in this "fourth arm" of marketing.

At the first conference our star speaker was Barry Gill, an Englishman who administers several million pounds' worth of sponsorship monies. He told how Durex, the leading British maker of condoms, came to him to see if they could make their product a household word without the snigger several generations of pubescent youth had attached to it.

He explained that a Formula One racing car, painted silver-grey, would have the right phallic look to it and the sport enough macho image to commend itself to young men. The Durex team was then put in place, and it actually won a race or two. In the sports pages, therefore, Durex became a common word.

When the team was disbanded, its mission for Durex accomplished, the company ran double-page spreads in all the quality Sundays with a picture of the winning car, Durex, on its side as the sponsor. Underneath was the phrase: "Durex, the small-family car."

If Durex could sponsor Formula One, anyone, said Gill, could sponsor anything. When later that year I saw *Kiss of the Spiderwoman*, a graphic homosexual play in Edmonton's Citadel Theatre, sponsored by the accounting firm Clarkson Gordon, I thought we were getting somewhere.

Canada was, in fact, part of a worldwide movement towards more private funding of the arts. In the United Kingdom the Association for Business Sponsorship of the Arts was set up, very much on the CBAC model, and I attended its opening meeting in the Royal Academy in London. Its founding director, Luke Rittner, later to head the Arts Council of Great Britain, and I would often find each other at conferences around the globe in countries wanting to get on the bandwagon.

In Stockholm we attended a meeting called by Enskilda Banken to explore how business could get more involved with arts being slowly strangled for funds in Sweden. That was the meeting where the minister for culture attended at the first session to say it could not and would not be allowed.

"Don't listen too hard to him," a Swedish colleague said. "His majority in government is maintained only by partly Communist support. He was talking to them this morning, not us."

In Paris, where UNESCO convened a similar conference on what they called patronage, an expatriate Hungarian printmaker living in Tuxedo Junction, New York, astonished everyone by producing a beautiful print for each delegate. "You have a gift from me on your table," he said. "I have been here for four days and heard only talk. No one has offered any patronage. I am the only patron: the print is yours. Remember, it is always the artist who ultimately subsidizes the arts. Collectively the creators are, as well, the patrons."

In Vancouver, during Expo 86, at Versailles convened by the French government, in London, in New York, Luke and I would meet, each time allowing that though the arts and business were not out of the woods yet, we had made progress towards a substantial clearing.

For fifteen years it seemed that I was present at every significant advance in the arts in Canada, whether in the opening of a new facility, the creation of a new company or festival, the launching of a new initiative or, especially in the seventies, the announcement of a new art collection to be purchased for a new headquarters building.

This last activity was sometimes entrusted to an art consultant like Nina Kaiden Wright or Jeanne Parkin, who planned the collections of such companies as Cadillac-Fairview and Reid Paper International. Sometimes, however, it was given to a committee of employees with power to co-opt professional advice. This sometimes had unforeseen results.

A woman on the Shell Canada committee, which spent $500,000 on buying works for their new Calgary headquarters, confronted the chairman of the committee one morning. "You SOB. Since you put me on this committee, you've cost me hundreds of dollars."

"How come?"

"When I joined, I had nice pictures in my apartment and a super cut-velvet picture over my bed. I now know that the pictures were chocolate-box and the velvet — yech. I've pitched them all, and it's costing me a fortune to replace them with what I now think good. And Shell corporate relations doesn't underwrite me!"

Even being highly selective in my travelling and, by now, sharing some of it with Sarah Iley, it was all exhilarating but exhausting. At least corporations and arts people alike respected it, used it, and collaborated more than they ever had before. It was even noticed in academe when Professor Samuel Martin, the acknowledged authority on corporate philanthropy, wrote in his book *An Essential Grace* (1985):

> *Edinborough is the council's president and chief executive officer, a post he has held since its inception. British-born and Cambridge-educated, he exudes what one might expect from a cultured, dedicated arts protagonist. He travels, lectures, confers, promotes, and writes at a breathtaking pace. Perhaps his most gruelling labour is the column he writes regularly for* The Financial Post *— a thousand words a week covering a wide range of cultural topics varying from philosophy to economics. For more than a decade Edinborough's column has added a touch of elegance to a publication dedicated to pragmatic business*

reporting, and has enriched Canadians' understanding of the diversity and quality of artistic expression in their country.

Gruelling labour? No way. I was doing what I wanted to do under the most generous and open circumstances a man could have. I could call any arts group in the country and ask for tickets at a moment's notice. Executive offices were open to me. And I was riding a tidal wave of creative activity and public acceptance of it such as this country had never seen before. Adrenaline flowed in a similar tidal wave in my system. Just how much I did not realize until, in August 1989, I retired from CBAC and relinquished my column in *The Financial Post*.

It was like having been on the first Everest climb, or part of Canada's winning downhill ski team: you were history in the making. One hoped that oneself would not so quickly become history, though.

For an immigrant whose roots were still deep in another country, it was even more affecting. The land had indeed proved bright.

How bright was made most evident by a gala organized to mark my retirement. Orchestrated by Eileen Love and Sarah Iley, it brought together over eight hundred people from business and the arts. The ballroom of the Sheraton Centre in Toronto was made over into a dinner theatre. Grace was sung in Latin by the Toronto Boys Choir under Ned Hanson. The Twenty-sixth Royal Canadian Artillery Band played for dancing. Anne of Green Gables came from Charlottetown to sing, as did a couple from the Canadian Opera Company. The Arete Physical Mime Troupe from Calgary and the Robert Desrosiers dancers from Toronto put on vivid shows. John Kimura Parker played two brilliant Chopin preludes to round it off. A special supplement was wrapped around that night's *Financial Post* with articles and messages from a variety of people. The one that underscored the spirit of the evening and, in a sense, pulled together my public life in

Canada was from Donald Fullerton, chairman, president, and CEO of the Canadian Imperial Bank of Commerce:

During my early banking career I was fortunate to have been given the opportunity to work in a variety of locations across Canada which brought me into contact with what I thought was almost every type of human being — from penny stock promoters on Bay Street to fishermen at Ucluelet on Vancouver Island.

So in 1960 when I received the prestigious appointment to the preeminent branch of the then Bank of Commerce at Bay and Richmond (City Hall Branch), I felt very comfortable with my ability to cope not only with balance sheets, but with a wide spectrum of people and opportunities that no doubt existed in such a key location.

It was not hard to isolate the promoters, develop an understanding of the inventory procedures of Spadina Avenue, and generally find my way around the halls of high finance.

However, the longer I stayed at the branch, the more intrigued I became of a rather high-profile account which seemed to be managed in defiance of all the natural financial laws of "gravity."

I was aware this company had gone through a number of CEOs until finding one who had such a meagre knowledge of finance as to be comfortable while balancing between bankruptcy and brilliance.

I set out deliberately to get to know this CEO, or whatever the title was at that time, and I must admit it was worth every minute of the time spent.

Not only did I have the pleasure of getting to know a man of many talents — some literary — but more importantly I learned a lesson that has served me well in my banking career.

When politicians, civil servants, company officials, and some bankers were saying in unison Dome Petroleum was dead, I was reflecting on city hall days and Arnold Edinborough, and thinking how would he have dealt with this problem.

If the boat truly was sinking, the obvious answer was to continue to clamber up to the high side. It might well float for longer than anyone thought possible. If it eventually was going down, it is relatively easy to jump clear from the high side. If you were watching closely, you will have observed one RDF employing the Edinborough technique as the Dome floated longer than anyone, except Arnold and I, thought possible.

It was a night to remember, and it *will* be remembered, since the proceeds from it have endowed a series of annual forums in my name that will try to bring sound advice and missionary fervour to the medium tier of business and the smaller arts groups in their own communities. Already such forums have been held in Kingston, Ontario; Victoria and Kelowna in British Columbia; and Edmonton in Alberta. Though not the sparkling occasions that great night in October 1989 was, they have brought together business and the arts in a meaningful community spirit and will continue to do so. Their establishment, in fact, really tops off what I and a dedicated board and staff had worked so long and pleasurably to bring about.

XXI

OF VISIONS
AND FRIENDS

L OOKING BACK OVER IT ALL," ASKS Tish, "would you do it
   again?"

That is not easily answered. Hypothetical questions never are.
But there are major decisions that can be reviewed in the light of
subsequent events and judged.

First, coming to Canada. That was a right decision. I love
England. I love her history and the incredible beauty of the
countryside. I know that the education I had, both at the local
grammar school, at Cambridge, and in the army (a great learning
experience, that) was in every way excellent. A system based, as it
was, on rhetoric, logic, and grammar has stood me in good stead
ever since. And that is not to make a covert comparison with
Canadian education. I grew up without television in a rural
community. I thus had time to be educated when young, and
Cambridge always gave its students, wherever they came from,
time to learn.

But a career in England — at least a career in the university —
was made difficult by a still quite strong cliquishness. England was
not a closed shop for talent, but it did put false barriers in the way
when I graduated.

In Canada, as G. B. Harrison so rightly said, there was an
openness, a welcome for energy, initiative, and talent that was

warmer, more flexible, and which, therefore, offered more opportunities.

And Queen's University, particularly, gave as equal an opportunity to its newcomers as to its established people. Teaching is second nature to me. I cannot see a person in a car looking at a map without offering help to find out where he wants to go. My rural upbringing still makes me greet any person I meet on a nonbusy street. The urge to communicate is deep within me. So, though I originally came on a two-year contract, there was no hesitation about taking tenure and deciding to stay when the time came. I had willing students and, very soon, eager listeners outside the classroom.

The year back at Cambridge from 1952 to 1953 showed me that my apprehension about the semiclosed shop was right. It also showed me that all the venerable trappings of the Senior Common Room, the ancient customs, and the solid tradition were still aimed at the unmarried don living in college in a sort of medieval cocoon. Leaving all that history and tradition, which has deep personal resonance for me, was difficult and I still react to it almost physically even after what Margaret Thatcher has done to it.

Leaving the university for journalism? Again, right. I like to feel in the middle of things, and editing a newspaper or magazine certainly put me there. I have often thought, in a sudden flash, of how extraordinary it was for me — an immigrant — to be at the Press Gallery Dinner in Ottawa or in the back room with Robert Thompson, arguing about foreign policy when he was elected head of the Social Credit Party, or giving a newsclip on television about national policy in the Pearson-Diefenbaker years.

I always wanted to write. Was journalism the answer? Would I have been able to do what a Cambridge acquaintance has done: retire to a Greek island, write a novel or two, and live off reviews? I don't think so. Malcolm Muggeridge maintained that journalism destroyed a writer. For me it created one. Not a writer's writer.

But then I would not have been a writer in the sense that Robertson Davies or Mordecai Richler are writers, anyway. (And they have both been journalists, as well.)

The Council for Business and the Arts plus the weekly *Financial Post* column, and the monthly column in the *Canadian Churchman* (now the *Anglican Journal*) gave me the discipline of deadlines with privileged access not at all available to other writers on cultural affairs.

Saturday Night I would do differently. I made the cardinal error of mixing my personal money with that of a business. Though the experience of *Saturday Night* and its scope were greatly rewarding, the end result was financial disaster. The losses I sustained over *Saturday Night* took every nickel I ever made in this country. It gave me rich experiences then; it has robbed me of security now.

And what did it all achieve for *Saturday Night* in the long run? The continuity of a magazine whose time was probably gone. National consensus through intelligent periodical commentary is no longer a realistic objective.

What about CBAC? It certainly helped to make Canada aware of its creative talent. It helped to establish levels of funding that guaranteed high standards of performance both from the creative artist and the interpretative ones.

But as for welding Canada together, it is difficult to say that it achieved anything. Canada is now fractured and fractious. A government mired in patronage and parish pump politics, helpless in the face of organized business and a politically ebullient Quebec, has, through its cutting back on the CBC, through its emasculation of the National Arts Centre, and its craven submission to vocal and violent minority groups, destroyed the Canada we came to forty years ago. One can only hope — and I do hope — that there is enough substance in the cultural explosion to bring the country back to its manifest destiny of being the relatively tolerant, hardworking, tough-minded, opportunistic country that it once was. A country proud of its history of nonviolence and too modest about its achievements in science, public policy, and international peacekeeping.

Where there is no vision the people perish. And since the politicians of the old school have no vision, let us hope, and I reiterate that I do hope, that among the writers and thinkers and performers who have flourished so notably in the past forty years, a vision will be found and set high before us all.

But life is not lived all the time on a public level, and the fabric of our private lives has always been a varied and fascinating weave in this still-new country of ours.

Friends for one part. It is often said that friends are not truly made after school or university. Or, to put that another way, the friends made in college and school are the ones who last through life. Certainly the friends Tish and I made there are still close to us. Sometimes, because we live three thousand miles apart, we don't see them for years together. Yet when we had a three-month celebratory visit to the U.K. after my retirement from CBAC, we picked up exactly where we left off in household after household. It is really Tish who has kept the lines open — letters and Christmas cards every year. But the warmth of these friends, still curious as to our transatlantic lives, was a tremendous tonic to us.

But in Canada we also have friends who have been supporters and encouragers and always there. The lives of Robertson and Brenda Davies, through the *Kingston Whig-Standard* and *Saturday Night*, have been fairly entwined with ours. Rob's toasts to our daughter Sarah (his goddaughter) on her twenty-first birthday and her marriage were models of affectionate meretriciousness. As Sarah said in response to the twenty-first birthday toast, "Everybody — well, almost everybody — in this room knows that my godfather is Canada's leading practitioner of fiction. And boy! have you just seen him at work!"

Jack and Peggy Seed, Jack as the patient secretary and director of Saturday Night Publications Limited, Peggy as the benevolent owner of the farmhouse in which the bulk of this book has been written. Deep in the Big Head River Valley, just a few steps from the Bruce Trail, Little Hills is the third in our rural retreats.

The first was Garden Island, owned by the Calvin family — a nineteenth-century paradise still functioning as a twentieth-century summer place. The second was Fraser House, one of Jim Walker's properties between Claremont and Uxbridge — an old small farmhouse set in plantations of red oak and white pine.

Little Hills, like the other two, brings me back to my rural roots. A farmer born is a farmer all his life, and accepted as such. It was a great moment for me when Milford Sewell, my farm neighbour in the valley, asked me on my return from a four-day conference on theatre in the heart of London, how the crops were shaping up in England.

Garden Island was the longest of our tenancies — thirty-two summers — and it shaped our family's whole attitude to the Canadian tradition.

The island residents themselves were an intriguing community: Ken McNaught, professor of history at the University of Toronto and biographer of J. S. Woodsworth; Donald Swainson, professor of history at Queen's and biographer of Sir John A. Macdonald; Eric Harrison and his wife, Elizabeth — he a historian and military writer, she a successful painter; George Whalley, professor of English at Queen's, who burrowed endlessly into the Coleridge notebooks at a huge harvest table in the back half of his cottage; Lorne McDougall, conservative economist and economics consultant to the Canadian Pacific Railway; plus various members of the Calvin family.

In Toronto Paul Deacon and Adele: Paul who became an associate when I started my *Financial Post* column during his term as editor; Lyman Henderson, patron of the arts and the giver of the annual New Year's Eve party that we attended for thirty years until our own extended families took precedence.

Frank McEachren, who with his wife, introduced us to the Ceilidh, where in the now-demolished armories on University Avenue we met monthly to dance Scottish reels for fifteen minutes, recover for refreshments for fifteen minutes, and so on for three hours, the pipers wailing all the time. (Tish is the Macdonald and Scottish. I, through my name, was allowed as a bastard Scot.)

It was Frank who nominated me to the Massey Hall board, which in itself, as we built Roy Thomson Hall, was one of the great experiences of my life in Canada. Building through the CBAC was one thing; building an actual building was another, especially when it has the serene and imposing presence in the downtown as Roy Thomson Hall does.

John Gellner, fellow immigrant, whose career as a journalist was started at *Saturday Night* when he retired at fifty-two from the RCAF. We lunched alternately at the Royal Canadian Military Institute and the Albany Club every week for years. And how much I have learned from a man who grew up under the Austro-Hungarian emperor (his grandfather was port commandant at Trieste), helped build a democratic Czechoslovakia, served as a bomber pilot on innumerable raids over Germany in the war, and retired as director of strategic studies at York University and founding editor of the *Canadian Defence Quarterly*.

When we came back to Canada after our three-month English trip, we picked up with these friends in just the same way as we had done with those in the U.K.

A life of warm friendship. A life with a quirky but devoted family, all of whom have gone their own less than conservative way — the proprietor of a restaurant, the proprietor of a ballet-theatre school (without a nickel of subsidy, she fiercely states), and an inheritor (and part creator) of the CBAC tradition.

And a life blessed with a rich, supportive, endlessly nurturing marriage with a woman whose interweaving into the Canadian scene was, by definition, less than her partner's. Though we have travelled together a good deal, the Canada I know, from Stephenville to Nanaimo and up to Inuvik and Yellowknife, is not the one she knows.

Every Christmas for years now we have given a programme of readings in which she reads *The Journey of the Magi*. As she read it this year, I thought how appropriate for her time in Canada were the lines:

> *A cold coming we had of it*
> *Just the worst time of the year*
> *For a journey, and such a long journey*
> *. . . [but] we continued*
> *And arrived at evening, not a moment too soon*
> *Finding the place; it was, you may say, satisfactory.*

Satisfactory, indeed, and thank God the journey now so well accompanied and with such a trail of memories is not yet over. We are still healthily, happily, on the road.

INDEX